'My Africa'

The inside story of sixty years of this world-renowned institution, written from the unique viewpoint of a young girl living and growing up in Sir Peter Chalmers Mitchell's dream of an open-plan Zoo Park, the first of its kind in this country. Her father was the Resident Engineer who took her to Whipsnade Park just before it opened, thus leading her into an enchanted childhood.

As well as tracing the Park's full history, the book is full of anecdotes, both humorous and tragic, about its animals and people – all of whom she has known down the years. Despite eventually moving away in adult life, her enduring love affair with the place never faltered. She has felt impelled to return again and again to follow its changing fortunes.

In the last pages she expresses the hope and belief that, with its primary aim, as always, the preservation of near extinct species, Whipsnade Wild Animal Park will go on into the next century and far beyond.

Over 130 drawings and rare photographs, mostly unpublished, add a further fascinating dimension to this inspiring story.

"A pioneer of its kind in a zoo world full of bars and concrete, Whipsnade showed the way animals could and should be kept. Long may it prosper."

Gerald Durrell

To Valerie Warren

Best wishes

Luy Pendr

Whipsnade

Wild Animal Park

'My Africa'

by
Lucy Pendar

Introduction
by
Gerald Durrell

As a child Whipsnade was my Africa – my Asia – Canada – Australia – in fact, the whole world encompassed in some 500 acres on a Chiltern hill.

First published March 1991
by
The Book Castle
12 Church Street
Dunstable
Bedfordshire LU5 4RU

Cover design incorporates a specially commissioned painting by Bill Pendar

ISBN 1 871199 65 4 (paperback)
ISBN 1 871199 80 8 (hardback)

Computer Typeset by 'Keyword', Aldbury, Herts
Printed and bound by Hartnoll Ltd., Bodmin

INTRODUCTION
by
Gerald Durrell

When I was a child I was lucky enough to be brought up on the Greek island of Corfu. In those days - before the introduction of the detrimental insecticides and the all-destroying tourist boom - this enchanted island was a paradise for wildlife and so I caught and kept a menagerie of creatures. I made valiant attempts to confine these to my bedroom, but on more than one occasion they escaped and caused havoc, for my family were not as zoologically orientated as I was, and so the scattering of a matchbox full of scorpions among them as they sat at a meal had an electric effect.

But my bedroom teemed with strange creatures, praying mantis with their prim, evil little faces and bulbous eye, tree frogs that looked as if carved out of jade, huge warty toads with great golden eyes, Squirrel dormice, shrews, sea horses and slugs, and outside in the garden a host of birds such a hoopoes, kestrels, magpies and seagulls, to say nothing of my three dogs and a donkey. I had, by that time, decided what I wanted to do in life. I wanted to travel the world collecting animals for zoos and, later, to establish a zoo of my own.

When we returned to England I realised that, if I was to achieve my ambitions, it was necessary for me to have experience with creatures larger than scorpions and sea horses, so I applied for and, to my astonishment, got a job at Whipsnade. I was the lowest of the low, the relief keeper. It was Geoffrey Vevers, then Superintendent of London Zoo, who, when he gave me my final reference, thought up the grandiose title of 'Student Keeper'. However, being the relief keeper suited me very well for I went on the various sections to help out when people had their days off or sick leave. Thus, one minute I would be helping to deal with lions and tigers and the next day perhaps zebra and gnus or cranes and geese or - best of all - the creature I fell irrevocably in love with, the giraffe. Its enormous but elegant body, its strange silence, its huge liquid eyes, with eyelashes as thick as an Astrakhan rug, and its long blue tongue, all went to make one of the strangest and most beautiful animals on earth, whose disappearance from this planet would be more terrible than losing a Rembrandt or the Acropolis. So my time at Whipsnade was, from my point of view, very well spent and stood me in good stead in the future.

A pioneer of its kind in a zoo world full of bars and concrete, Whipsnade showed the way animals could and should be kept and what all zoos should endeavour to emulate. Long may it prosper.

Gerald Durrell
2nd August 1990

FOREWORD
by
Andrew Forbes
Chief Executive, Whipsnade Wild Animal Park

Since opening in May 1931, over thirty million people have passed through the gates of Whipsnade to visit the collection of rare and increasingly endangered species that find the Park safe refuge from the pressures that the human race imposes on the natural world.

Many changes have taken place physically within the Park over the years. However, the original aims conceived by the Zoological Society of London have not been compromised. Whipsnade Wild Animal Park plays a major role in increasing man's knowledge and understanding of animals.

It is fitting that the book has been written by a lady who has solid ties with Whipsnade, as she was actually brought up in the Park. The book covers Whipsnade's history since before its inception in 1931 to the present day, and a look into the future. It is also pleasing that the book has been published at a time when the Park will be celebrating another milestone in its history – its Diamond Jubilee.

Andrew Forbes
11th September 1990

ACKNOWLEDGEMENTS

My grateful thanks are due to Gerald Durrell for the Introduction to this book and Andrew Forbes, the Chief Executive of Whipsnade Wild Animal Park, for the Foreword. To Lord Zuckerman, for his initial encouragement, Reg Fish, the Librarian and Archivist of the Zoological Society of London, John Buckledee, Editor of the Luton News and Dunstable Gazette, and to all the staff at Whipsnade, from its Managers to its newest recruits who have been so generous in their forbearance and with their anecdotes and stories. Particularly I must thank Owen Chamberlain, John and Christa Datlen, for their assistance throughout my research, Graham Lucas, Pete Williams and Bob Wingate for their co-operation especially at the beginning and Paul Bowes for agreeing to publish and his unfailing friendly encouragement.

Lucy Pendar
September 1990

CHAPTERS

KEY TO ILLUSTRATIONS

My thanks to all who kindly assisted with photographs.

BP	Bill Pendar
BT	Bruce Turvey
DG	Dunstable Gazette – Home Counties Newspapers Ltd
DP	Derick Pendar
GB(i)	1932 Guide Book
GB(ii)	1939 Guide Book
GB(iii)	1973 Guide Book
GS	George Sandifer
JD	John Datlen
JH	Julie Heard
JS	John Skeaping
LB	Laura Beal
LM	Louise Meara
LMAG	Luton Museum & Art Gallery
MT	By kind permission of the Marquess of Tavistock and the Trustees of the Bedford Estate
MW	Maureen White
UEA	University of East Anglia
WSB	'The Whipsnade Zoo & Its Inmates', by W S Berridge FZS
ZO	Zoo Operations Ltd

CHAPTER 1

The Dream

Whipsnade has always been magical for me. It was the golden place of my childhood, where I wove fantasies as I wandered through its woods and glades or sat on the banks of its enchanting pools.

My childhood was filled with the roar of lions, tigers slinking through their overgrown jungle of a den, polar bears splashing in their pond on sunny summer days or rolling in deep snow in winter time, American bison wandering across the great downland paddock by the side of the road which was to become known as Bison Hill. Wallabies, Chinese water deer and muntjacs running free. The trumpeting of elephants – the barking of sea lions – wolves howling in the dark wood at the bottom of my garden – the constant cry of peacocks. The whole world around me – encompassed in some 500 acres on a Chiltern hill.

My parents took me to Whipsnade in a removal van. In the days before ordinary people owned motor-cars, it was usual to travel in the pantechnicon, alongside their possessions, when moving house. So that was how we left London one foggy morning in November 1929.

The fog persisted as, leaving St Albans, the van chugged along the Watling Street and turned into Bucket Lane. My mother told me that there was an eerieness in journeying through the gloomy countryside not knowing where she was going, but, by the time the van emerged from the overhanging tunnel of trees, the sun had burned through the blanket of fog and I entered a golden Whipsnade, fast asleep on my mother's lap. My mother's cries of delight and surprise, at the scene around us, soon woke me up.

Cows grazed placidly on the lush green grass, now bathed in sunlight. Smoke rose from the tiny cottages, nestling behind their tidy hedges. The fairytale sight of our new home – a little pointed roofed, red-brick house, silhouetted against dark, sombre pine trees was just like a picture in my pop-up nursery rhyme book. To my mother, it was indeed a fairytale come true. A house of our very own, instead of three rooms on the top floor of Uncle Alf's Victorian terrace villa in

Camden Town. Huge iron gates swung open as the removal van conveyed us into the near-derelict estate that was destined to become one of the most famous places in the world.

My father, Albert Corbett, had looked after the boilers and filtration plant in the Aquarium at the London Zoo. For the past three years, the whole place had buzzed with Dr Peter Chalmers Mitchell's latest brain child. He was a lively, enthusiastic Scot, who'd been called in to become the Secretary to the Zoological Society of London when it had faced bankruptcy in 1903. He'd pulled it back into profit, not only by sorting out its affairs, but, with some of his innovative ideas, such as the Mappin Terraces. This structure was a ferro-concrete pseudo mountain. Goats climbed over the top section, lower down, bears could be viewed over a low barrier across a ditch, in 'rock' strewn lairs. To save space, always at a premium in Regent's Park, the inside of the 'mountain' was hollow and housed a magnificent Aquarium. He had persuaded Mr Mappin of the famous London Jewellers, Mappin & Webb, a Fellow of the Society, to finance the project and people had flocked to see and enjoy this new idea, despite the fact that, by the time it was completed, World War I had started.

The Mappin Terraces, Regent's Park London, 1990. The huge rock-like structure in the background was completed during the first World War. For the first time animals were exhibited in this country against a pseudo natural background instead of in cages.

/DP

2

His latest project, to celebrate the Society's Centenary, was to take the Mappin Terrace concept a stage further by creating a country Zoo Park, where all the animals could be in, as near as possible, natural surroundings, instead of barren cages. After a long search, by 1929, the Hundredth Anniversary of the granting by King George IV of the Royal Charter, he'd found the site for his dream, in a derelict farm in Bedfordshire! Work was already under way.

Now, some of the senior posts were to be filled by staff from the London Zoo and my father had been approached to become the Resident Engineer. Since 'Resident' meant a house with the job, there was really no choice. It would mean he'd have to give up his swimming and his boxing, my mother would have to leave her mother and sister and forego her visits to the pictures and the Music Hall. But, they would have a house with a garden – and how much better for me! Not yet two, I'd already had bronchitis – brought on by the dank London air. Now, I could live in the country, have grass to play on instead of pavements, fields instead of streets.

At last, the long tiring moving day was over and, with me snugly tucked up in my cot, my parents sat by the fire sipping tea and wondered what, exactly, they had done.

The Gate Cottages on the right silhouetted against the dark pine trees of the Old Wolf Wood. /GB(i)

My mother hadn't expected a coal-fired range ... She only hoped she'd be able to cook on it ...! Then, there was the problem of buying food ...! The nearest shops were three miles away! True, there was a bus from Studham to Dunstable, but they would need to walk at least half a mile to the cross-roads to catch it and it only ran on Wednesdays and Saturdays ...! Mrs Macdonald, who'd moved into the cottage next door, with her Head Keeper husband, two weeks previously, told her that some tradesmen called two or three times a week and the milkman came every day. Everything would need such careful planning. No popping out to the corner shop for items forgotten.

There wasn't any electricity either ...! Although there was promise that it would come soon. Some of the more eminent villagers had protested that the pylons would spoil the environment – but an Inquiry had gone against them and it would probably be laid on by the end of the year. Still, the soft yellow glow of the oil lamp spilling over the room was comforting as she sat wondering about our future, listening to the eerie whispering of the trees as the November night wind brushed them against each other in the darkness outside.

It had been on another such November day, three years earlier, that another party had set off from London in the fog. This party had consisted of members of the Council of the Zoological Society, a group of distinguished gentlemen, some of whom were not at all anxious to make the thirty-mile journey through the fog. But Peter Chalmers Mitchell was not a man to be deterred. Making a telephone call to a friend in the Chilterns, he established that the fog was nowhere near as bad in the country. Re-assured, the convoy of sedate limousines set out for Bedfordshire. Taking the route through Watford and Hemel Hempstead, rather than the Watling Street, they arrived at the Dagnall end of Hall Farm Estate.

Sir Peter Chalmers Mitchell, CBE FRS DSc LID 1864–1945, Secretary Zoological Society 1903–1935, the man who dreamed of a Wild Animal Park. /ZO

By now, the sun was breaking through and, leaving their cars, they were soon walking on open downland, seven hundred feet above sea level. A breeze blew from behind them as they walked and the sun, having burned away the last remnants of the fog, poured its warmth on them. Wisps of mist still lingered round homesteads and hedgerows in the valley beneath, but, above, the sky was blue, and excited expectancy hung on the downland air.

It took them the best part of an hour to walk the length and breadth of the land that was for sale. They saw the old farmhouse which Peter envisaged as the main Restaurant and inspected the nearby lone cottage, which would house the Superintendent. Making their way along the little footpaths that criss-crossed the estate, they realised that many of these were public Rights of Way, which would be lost once the farmland was fenced in. An Act of Parliament would be necessary to alter these. They passed an isolated wood of oak, hazel and cherry trees rising above rhododendron and dying bracken. Through tangled elder and brambles they came to another woodland area of tall, dark, conifers – pine and the gentler larch. The ground beneath their passing feet soft from the endless years of fallen needles. Emerging from the gloomy wood, they came, once more, into the sunlight on the downlands' edge near an enchanting little pool called Ouseley Pond. Peter likened it to a fairy mirror which reflected the tall reeds at its edge and the taller fir trees behind. On the banks of this pool, which in spring would be awash with primroses and daffodils, the Council made the unanimous decision to purchase the Whipsnade estate.

John Spedan Lewis, the heir to John Lewis's the famous London store, did not want things to be held up. He promised that, if the Private Member's Bill they needed to alter the Rights of Way failed to get through Parliament, he would take the land off the Society's hands. With that assurance, Peter Chalmers Mitchell purchased the four hundred and eighty odd acres of the Freehold property of Whipsnade Estate for £13,480.12s.10d. in December 1926.

But, before the work could begin, he had to placate the locals. One Parish Council claimed the right to dig for flints over twenty acres of land they would now lose. A stretch of land, sheltered from the westerly winds by a great hawthorn hedge, had been a camp site for generations of gypsies. People came from far afield, even as far as London, to dig ferns for sale. Local churches cut holly for their Christmas decorations. Villagers gathered blackberries. All this would end ...

And, then there was their fear ... Inhabitants of nearby villages were very apprehensive about lions and tigers, wolves and bears, roaming the hillside. Peter assured them that the entire estate would be enclosed by a nine foot fence with an inward-facing overhang. No animals would be able to get out. His commonsense, his charm and the whole attitude of his approach won them all over.

He felt the time had come to make a start ... Organising his work

'They carved exploratory paths through tangled brambles.' /BP

load in London to leave his weekends free, Peter would tear down to Whipsnade at the wheel of his fast car, his colleague Geoffrey Vevers in the passenger seat at his side. Together, armed with handsaws and axes, they carved exploratory paths through tangled brambles, hacked at the jungle of overgrown elder deciding which hedgerows should go – where plantations needed planting – opening up panoramic vistas.

The whole area was aerially photographed so that routes for the main avenues could be established. This in itself was an unusual event in the 1920's, but Peter Mitchell was well acquainted with flying. In 1920 he'd been the independent observer on the Air Ministry's survey of the possible air route from Cairo to the Cape. In his autobiography, 'My Fill of Days', he describes vividly the harrowing experiences of flight over Africa in early aircraft.

A gang of local labourers followed in the wake of the energetic Scot and his companion, widening the paths they cut, clearing the dead wood and rubbish. For rubbish lay around in abundance, dumped by campers, picnickers and villagers alike. Bonfires burned continuously, night and day.

In the early summer, Peter brought a group of friends from the London office to see the Society's acquisition. The smell of newly mown hay wafted from the fields as they settled themselves on the springy, downland turf. Once again, the sun shone as they turned to their picnic of cold chicken and salmon, washed down, as the young scientist with them recalled, by a fine Rhine wine. As this young scientist, Solly Zuckerman, recently over from South Africa, sat with Peter's Secretary, Miss Gay, F W Bond, the Society's Accountant, and Dr Geoffrey Vevers Superintendent of the London Zoo, he could have had no notion that one day he would be in Peter's shoes. That, in his time, he would become the Secretary of the Zoological Society of London and later its President, an office then held by the Duke of Bedford.

6

Enthusiastically, Peter told them of his plans – for lions and tigers in dells in the chalk pits that lay on the side of the downs – of zebra and antelope grazing freely in a single paddock, larger than the whole area of the London Zoo. He said he saw Whipsnade as one of three ways of preserving an already dwindling natural resource of wild animals. In the Transvaal, lions were nearly extinct. Hyaenas, were being trapped – poisoned and shot out of existence. Giraffe – rhino – buffalo *would*, in fact, *be* extinct by the following year. Mountain zebra – red hartebeeste – and bontebok were so rare that they had almost been exterminated.

To him the purchase of Whipsnade was the Society's most valuable achievement. But, nonetheless, he knew there would be pitfalls. Novelties fade quickly. Whipsnade's development could only evolve slowly. He knew that there would be temptations, particularly financial ones. Some would prefer a quick success! But that must not be ... The whole development of the project must be gradual. It required a faith to be maintained, despite past failed experiments or unseen difficulties. The whole concept of Whipsnade had to be viewed in the 'time warp' of the Society, not by the limited life span of the individual.

At first, he'd wanted to call the estate 'The Chiltern Animal Park', for, as he said, there was no reason to associate the venture with Whipsnade any more than Studham or Dagnall. There were, after all, four entrances planned. One at the bottom of the downs – the Icknield Gate, one at Whipsnade and one at each of the other two villages.

In fact, Peter envisaged the Main Entrance at Dagnall ... He was hoping the London, Midland & Scottish Railway Company would divert their Euston line at Berkhamsted or Boxmoor and run a link line into Dagnall. Here the main Avenue into the Zoo would be twenty feet wide. In the event, the railway line never came! Dagnall Gate never opened. The rain washed away the part-made road. The whole area of woody hill and downland flanking the derelict road remained the undeveloped area of the zoo ever after known as 'Sir Peter's Way'.

The bus Company, however, agreed to run a service from Luton railway station, via Dunstable, across the downs, through Whipsnade village to the Whipsnade Gate and so the park became 'Whipsnade Park Zoo' or, as we have known it since 1988, 'Whipsnade Wild Animal Park'.

The Private Member's Bill, which cost the Society £1,848, passed through both Houses of Parliament, receiving its Royal Assent on 2nd July 1928. Work could now begin in earnest.

As Peter Mitchell's right hand man, Geoffrey Vevers knew the task of finding the work force would fall upon his shoulders. He'd already engaged some local farm hands ... Tall, fair-haired Phil Bates had been working on Hill Farm, which had been sold. Well known, locally, for his ability to care for sick animals and with his natural affection for dumb creatures, he came seeking work at the new zoo. Interviewed by Geoffrey Vevers, Phil was told that, in spite of the arrival of a pair of muntjacs, several hog deer and three North American turkeys – gifts of the Duke of Bedford – there was a great deal of work to be done before the animals arrived in force. If, however, he was prepared to work on the boundary fence and the making of paddocks, there was a job to be had right away. Phil jumped at it. He went off whistling, as was his wont, to join the gang on the boundary fence; not realizing that, by the time he retired from the Society he'd joined that day, he would be its Senior Overseer with full responsibility for *all* its animals and keepers.

Bert Rogers stayed where he was! Having been employed at Hall Farm, he simply transferred his loyalties from the old owners to the new. From ploughing Spicer's Field, he would help to fence it in and, ultimately, care for the strange foreign animals that would roam in it. A long way, indeed, from the day that a pheasant, killed by a shooting party, had plopped at his feet. Burying it in a furrow and marking the spot, he continued following his team of horses up and down the field. At the end of the day, he retrieved his pheasant. The Rogers family enjoyed a tasty meal, never dreaming as they ate the unusual delicacy, that equally unusual black and white striped, horse-like animals would replace Bert's team in Spicer's Field ...

Frank Meakins came to work on the boundary fence too, with no idea that his destiny was to play a major part in the record-breaking breeding of Big Cats!

But it became increasingly obvious to Geoffrey Vevers that he would not find enough men locally for the immense task that lay ahead. The government of the day was greatly concerned about the wasted man power due to the recession. In an attempt to give men the dignity of finding work, the Ministry of Labour had devised a scheme whereby it would provide seventy-five percent of the cost of men's labour if anyone could find them work and the other twenty-five percent of their wages. Geoffrey and Peter decided to avail themselves of this scheme and they and the Ministry diverted unemployed miners from the Welsh valleys to the Chiltern Hills. The scheme cost the Zoological Society some £5,000 - £6,000 for labour, plus £700 - £800 for tools, huts, etc. The huts would later become animal sheds.

On the first Monday in February 1929, three gangs, comprising fifteen men and a ganger in each, started work at Whipsnade, followed, the following Monday, by another three gangs. The men were billetted in Luton ... Len Archer, a butcher's boy in West Street, Dunstable, at the time, still recalls hearing the lusty Welsh voices long before the lorries carrying them to the Zoo reached the crossroads at the top of Church Street. The crescendo was deafening as they passed him, leaning on his bicycle, and the strains of their singing could still be heard as the lorries turned up the hill to the downs.

In the Park they once again took up the tools of their trade. But they no longer hewed coal in the bowels of the earth. Now they dug gravel and scree, hacked away at chalk and flints, making pits for animals and roadways, flexing their muscles, in the clear downland air. Five hundred yards of Duke's Avenue, named after the Society's President, The Duke of Bedford. Seven hundred yards of Cut-Throat Avenue, named after the little wood through which the footpath from Whipsnade to Dagnall had passed. One thousand, five hundred yards of Escarpment, which ran along the top of the downs. Names still used for the roads today and with only a slightly altered bend here and a widening there, following, sixty years on, the lines made by the miners. Thus, many men found work and passed through the Parks' gates during the next couple of years - some staying on to join the 'firm'.

A well, capable of yielding five thousand gallons of water an hour, was sunk. Incidentally, having, down the years, transferred to the Water Board's supply, the Society is now, in 1990, pumping its own

With my father outside the pump house.

water again. Each time it is tested, as it must be, being consumed by the general public, as well as the animals, it is declared to be the purest water in the area! A reservoir was constructed to hold half a million gallons of water and pipes were laid to take supplies round the Park. A drainage plant, complete with sewage filters, discreetly screened by water-loving shrubs and trees, euphemistically called the 'Willow Lagoon', was created, attracting many visitors to its banks until the all-pervading smell caused them to beat a hasty retreat.

This also formed part of my father's domain. Our house was one of the pair of semi-detached cottages forming the Whipsnade Gate Lodge. Designed by E Guy Dowber, ARA, it was kept to the style of the original old farmhouse. The farmhouse and its outbuildings were converted into a catering complex. This complex contained an expensive Central Restaurant seating some fifty people, a lounge and American Bar and the Cloisters where cheaper lunches, dinners and teas could be purchased. The Cloisters – still there but now glassed in – opened onto ornamental gardens. There was a large kitchen; a separate patisserie, where meringues, chocolate eclairs and mouthwatering little iced cakes were made; a still room; a vast storeroom; a linen room (primarily for white tablecloths and large white napkins and bedding); sleeping quarters for single, male members of the catering staff; ladies' and gents' lavatories and flats for the Catering Manager and the Society's Secretary.

Here, Miss Joan Proctor would stay whilst recovering from her many illnesses. Her first connection with the Zoological Society had come about when she was asked to design and make pseudo rocks for the London Zoo Aquarium. She had succeeded in making it so beautiful that King George V and Queen Mary had personally congratulated her. She subsequently became the Zoo's Curator of Reptiles, designing a new Reptile House, where snakes and lizards, alligators and crocodiles, among others, were displayed imaginatively against decorative backgrounds.

With my mother. Hall Farm, the early Restaurant, now the DISCOVERY Centre, is in the background.

It was no surprise then that she was very excited by the prospect of a whole zoo complex laid out in natural surroundings! She gave the Whipsnade venture her enthusiastic support, helping Peter with plans for the layout of the Park. Using her architectural talents, she designed a bothy in the village, which comprised four cottages for married keepers and separate quarters for single ones. She kept this building, again, to the same style as Hall Farm and the Gate Cottages.

She also came up with a more practical plan for the original Whipsnade Gate entrance than Dowber's, giving more consideration to the visitors. It was very different from the one we see today. Then, the Gate House had a tall tower bearing a blue-faced clock - blue being the original 'Zoo Colour'. Continuing from the gate house there were four pairs of turnstiles, all under a red-tiled gabled roof. There was also storage space for push-chairs and wheel-chairs - very necessary in the times before cars were admitted daily. On either side of the Gate House were double iron gates. On one side giving entrance to the courtyard where visitors queued for the turnstiles, on the other entrance to the main park for vehicles. A board on the gate showed the times and prices of admission and there was a nearby kiosk.

The approach to the Park showing the old original boundary fence supplied by the Darlington Fencing Company, with the overhang turning in to prove to the local inhabitants that the inmates could not escape.

Central and Duke's Avenues converged at the Whipsnade Gate. Duke's Avenue led to the downs and Ivinghoe Gap, which gave a splendid view of the Beacon through a frame of tree trunks and arched branches. Half way along and to the right of Duke's Avenue, a bear pit was constructed which, at the time of writing, remains unchanged. A large area of bushes and scrub was fenced in on three sides, with great iron bars. This meant that visitors were on a level with the bears and close enough, behind the low mesh protective barrier, to get a good impression of their size. On the fourth side, near the pond, an elevated path ran between the Bear enclosure and Flint Pit Paddock. From this path, the bears could be seen over a low barrier. Lady Yule had donated £1,000 for the bear pit and this elevated path, which was named after her, was a vantage point from which, in the old days, when feeding the animals was allowed, the general public would bestow their benevolence on the bears. And how they did! Great was the sight to see. A row of bears lying on their backs on the sloping bank, feet in the air, bellies so full they could no longer move, gorged as they were on cream cakes, biscuits and buns thrown to them by visitors on a Bank Holiday or busy summer Sunday.

The old Main Entrance.   /WSB

In the very early days there were some sloth bears at Whipsnade – black bears with pinkish white muzzles – also Himalayan black bears. One of these got out of its enclosure the day it arrived. Quickly re-captured, it repeated the performance a few hours later. This time, it was at large for three days, being finally caught when Phil Bates, spotting it up a tree, blew his whistle and stood guard. One week later, it escaped again! Startled by the sudden crash of metal in the garden, my mother and I rushed to the bedroom window. There, in the garden, was a bear with its head in our overturned dustbin! This time the bear created havoc wherever it went, leaving the scene of chaos one step ahead of its pursuers. No wonder – since they were armed with pitchforks and brooms! It took my dad and Joan Proctor to outwit the animal. Begging a large tin of treacle from the Restaurant storekeeper, they spread it on the doorstep of the ladies' lavatories nearby, making a trail into the building, and then hid themselves and lay in wait in bushes close by. At long last, they heard snuffling and tensed in anticipation as the bear appeared and started licking the step. Would their plan succeed? The bear followed the treacle trail into the lavatories and they triumphantly slammed the door on it. This time, the bear was packed off back to the London Zoo, in disgrace.

But, for me, that was not the end of the story. Several days later, Sir Peter, as Dr Mitchell had now become – to everyone's delight – appeared at our garden gate. I stared wide-eyed, for the tall distinguished white-haired gentlemen had a teddy bear in his arms! My mother hurried to answer the door. 'This is for Maisie', he said, using my nickname, 'to remind her of her father's part in the capture of the bear.' I still have Teddy. He's threadbare – he's lost his growl – his bright glass eyes have long been replaced, but … he's very precious … For he reminds me of the kindly white-haired man whose dream was Whipsnade Park.

With Teddy, the only friend I had till I started school at five.

14

CHAPTER 2

The Dream Becomes a Reality – May 23rd 1931

Sir Peter soon realised that there was no way Whipsnade would be ready to open during the actual Centenary year. Spring 1931 seemed to be about the best he could project, but, since he'd been tossing the idea around in his head for twenty-odd years, a couple more wouldn't make much difference.

Born like Andrew Carnegie in Dumfermline, Scotland, Peter had been invited to the opening of Carnegie's Museum in the United States in 1907. He always seized the opportunity to visit zoos in his travels abroad and this time took in the Bronx Zoological Park while in New York. It was this park, with its wide open spaces for great herds of animals, that had sowed the seed that was to germinate in Whipsnade.

He also knew that, when Whipsnade Park did finally open, it would not be finished. For many years visitors would only see his dream in the making. He must have known it was unlikely that he himself would live to see his dream fulfilled. As he explained in the first Guide Book, the Society having spent £100,000 on the basic groundwork, Whipsnade could only be transformed into 'a Park for the breeding of Wild Animals and a Sanctuary for British Wild Birds and Plants' as other monies became available.

Sadly, the park did not become a sanctuary for wild plants. Sir Peter had hoped that, once safe from plundering, behind the boundary fence, the native plants of the chalk hills, rough woodland and upland pasture would again bloom freely. The beautiful purple Pasque flower, with its golden centre, which, by some miracle, knows exactly when to blossom although Easter is a moveable festival, had completely disappeared from the chalk hills. Just its name remained at Pascombe Pit on the Dunstable end of the Downs. Wild orchids were gone. Pale wood anemones, with their white faces and fragile stems were rare, as were the sturdy yellow cowslips. Primroses and daffodils had been relentlessly plucked from little woods where old footpaths wound through, and the bluebell carpets were threadbare from years of plundering as they struggled bravely to exist beneath the tall beeches. Ironically, it was the freedom given to some of the new inmates – the fluffy grey-brown wallabies, leaping on their strong back legs, feeding on the open grassland at night and resting on it by day, the muntjac, the little Asian barking deer with its tusk-like canine teeth, the Chinese water deer, the constant pecking of peafowl, pheasants and wild turkeys, that helped to shattter his floral dream.

Whipsnade did not become a sanctuary for wild plants, but its destiny was most certainly to fulfil the other part of the Zoological Act. For, beyond all doubt, it was to become a 'Park for the Breeding of Wild Animals'. And its first momentous birth took place in May 1930.

There were now only twelve months left to the scheduled opening. Work was going on at a frenzied pace. Six rain shelters were necessary for the unpredictable British weather as there were no animal houses for visitors to shelter in. Four of these shelters still stand.

Cut Throat, taking its name from the little wood behind it, which down the years has changed from Cut Throat to Cut Thro'it and back to Cut Throat again. As children, we were convinced a horrific death, either suicide or murder, had taken place in the little copse, and that blood and gore had spilled on the mossy bank beneath the hazel trees. We cycled past swiftly, yet we felt cheated in the years it was called Cut Thro'it. Three Way Shelter is exactly what its name suggests. It is a three-sided structure which, therefore, always offers shelter whichever wind prevails, a necessity since it stands on a bleak spot between the old Lay Meadow and Hall Craft Panorama. The other two shelters still in existence in their original places are Hall Craft, by the tigers' dell, and Duke's Shelter in Duke's Avenue.

Work continued on animal sheds, paddocks and kiosks. There are two remaining kiosks still on their original sites, Avenue, by the Railway, and Triangle. Both have been altered and rebuilt, Avenue as early as 1934. Eating habits have changed down the years. We no longer take leisurely afternoon teas of cucumber sandwiches and cakes at green tables on grassy lawns, served by waitresses in neat uniforms. Now we grab a pizza or a burger and eat at rough picnic benches or as we hurry on our way.

In the midst of all this active preparation a wombat was born. Not a very spectacular animal for such a distinction, yet it was these rodent-like Australian marsupials that scored three 'firsts' for Whipsnade. In their native environment they dig long underground

A wombat. The Australian rodent-like marsupial that scored three 'firsts' for Whipsnade.   /BP

tunnels, some reaching as much as ten feet (three metres) in length, where they shelter from the heat of the day and the cold of the night. Not surprisingly, the first pair to come to Whipsnade dug themselves out. Not only from their pen but out of the Zoo as well, tunnelling under the boundary fence. One was recaptured. One, sadly, Phil Bates told me, fell prey to the Hertfordshire Hounds. So, small and comparatively insignificant though they may be in the animal kingdom, they made the 'hat trick' at Whipsnade. The first of its very few great escapes; the first death of an escapee; and finally, one year before it opened, its first birth.

Soon after this the wolves bred and the year rolled on to the momentous day when the name 'Whipsnade' would be thrust upon an unsuspecting world, which was, nevertheless, ready for its first country Zoo.

By the 1930s the British people were becoming mobile. Many now had bicycles. Coach companies were expanding, running regular excursions to the seaside. They were easily persuaded to ring the changes and offer their passengers a visit to the country – to the new Zoo. Motor bikes were popular, with side cars attached; many small families travelled thus with ease and speed. Motor cars were being mass-produced. Since a day out, away from the cities and towns, was the 'in thing' there could not have been a better time for launching the Whipsnade enterprise, which was also to prove itself an excellent place for Sunday School trips and school outings alike.

To accommodate the visitors' varied modes of transport, a large car park was laid out on ground opposite the Main Gate, as the Whipsnade entrance had now become. Long wooden sheds were built with racks for bicycles. Shelters were made for the endless queues of bus and coach passengers; there was a kiosk offering chocolates, ice cream and cigarettes; there were petrol pumps, and even an attendant mechanic. Early vehicles were notoriously unreliable, many overheated in the struggle to climb up Bison Hill. Help was at hand!

Perhaps the factor most vital to Whipsnade's early success was that, unlike the London Zoo, it was never reserved exclusively for Fellows and their friends on Sundays. Since most people's weekends consisted of only Saturday afternoon and all day Sunday, such a restriction would have stifled Whipsnade at birth. It was a fortunate clause in the 'Act' which said that Whipsnade was to be open to the general public on Sundays and not to be reserved for Fellows on more than twelve days in any one year. The London Zoo, on the other hand, had been reserved entirely for its Fellows for almost its first twenty years of existence, only being forced, by financial difficulties, to admit the general public, and then only on Mondays! Eventually restrictions were waived, but Sundays were still kept for the select few on Sunday mornings until the 1950s!

The only places reserved for Fellows at Whipsnade were a small garden in front of the Restaurant leading down to the water garden, and the Fellows' Pavilion on the downs. This wooden building had been dismantled to make way for the new restaurant in the London Zoo. It was brought to Whipsnade and re-erected between Ivinghoe Gap and the Bison Paddock. Painted green, it was thatched to be in keeping with the other kiosks and the rain shelters. Here, Fellows of the Society and their guests met for morning and evening drinks at its bar and, on long hot summer afternoons, tea was served on the verandah overlooking Ivinghoe Beacon, Totternhoe Knolls, Edlesborough Church on its hill and the Vale of Aylesbury stretching as far as the eye could see.

After the War the Pavilion came down in the world. With its thatched roof replaced by sheets of corrugated iron it was relegated to the role of Parrot House! This change, as you can imagine, caused a great deal of ribald amusement among the staff, some even said that it wasn't really any change at all!! But the weather from the west finally rotted its timbers. The parrots were housed elsewhere, a silence replaced their screeching on the downs and the relic of pre-War splendour was finally removed. A smart rain shelter marks the place where the Fellows' Pavilion once stood. It is a spot where I love to picnic on 'Open Nights' bathed in the rays of the glorious setting sun.

But the snobbish element associated with Regent's Park completely passed Whipsnade by. It was a relaxed, happy place to work and play, a large estate supervised by its own genial, larger-than-life Superintendent, Captain Beal.

In the early days, Dr Geoffrey Vevers, London's Superintendent had run both establishments, actually moving into a cottage on the

Captain W P B Beal MRCVS.
Whipsnade's first
Superintendent 1931–1947.
/LB

Whipsnade Estate to keep an eye on things. But this couldn't last once the Park was open. Then it would be a full-time job for one man. So, in May 1930, along with the birth of its wombat, Whipsnade acquired the services of William P B Beal, recently retired Principal Army Veterinary Officer of the Gold Coast, who moved into the village with his wife Gladys and small son Billy.

Captain Beal, was, to me, an enormous man! Not only was he some six feet tall, taller than anyone I knew, save for the slim Phil Bates, who always walked with a slight stoop anyway as if apologising for his height; Captain Beal was also twenty stones in weight! The first time I saw him and heard his great booming voice, I was terrified and cried to be taken home. I was sure some great giant had crashed into my fairyland! And I didn't know then that there could be big friendly giants as well as evil ogres!

But, down the years, a big friendly man was exactly what he turned out to be. From behind round-rimmed spectacles, that always seemed too small for him, he supervised a Whipsnade that flourished happily; his staff soon learned that the 'Captain's bark was worse than his bite'. It became a big friendly estate. Even the men's annual Christmas Dinner seemed to savour of the Harvest Supper, as A G Street, who once visited Whipsnade, described so vividly in his book, 'Farmer's Glory'.

Perhaps the only time when the Captain and his staff were not relaxed was on the days of the monthly Whipsnade Committee meeting. They all knew they were doing their best. They hoped it would meet with approval. It was the one time the keepers stood to attention and touched their forelocks respectfully. The meetings were held in the Beals' drawing room, the Duke of Bedford having previously led the cavalcade of inspection in his big open-topped limousine, presiding. Sir Peter, Dr Vevers, Mr Alfred Ezra - a great

Herbrand, the 11th Duke of Bedford, President of the Zoological Society of London at the time of Whipsnade's creation. He commemorated the opening of the Park by planting a Beech tree at the Down's end of Duke's Avenue. The Duke's Beech is now a very fine tree.   /MT

benefactor down the years – Mr Spedan Lewis, among others, settled themselves in the large chintz-covered armchairs and were served tea from Mrs Beal's silver teapot and best bone china tea service. With the inspection over, the Committee gone, Whipsnade fell back into its pattern of happy, carefree living for another month.

By this time, there were forty-seven men employed besides the Heads of Departments, catering, office staff and gatekeepers. Four gardeners cut the grass and planted and tended the flower beds. Twelve men in the Works Department carried out building projects and general maintenance, whilst nine keepers cared for the animals and birds. There were, however, another twenty-two men who were partly employed in the Works Department, but who could also be called upon to don the smart uniform of grey jacket, riding breeches, black leather gaiters and peaked cap, to become supplementary keepers. No qualifications were needed for keepering then.

All the animals were reckoned to need was water, food and good clean stalls. So, anyone strong enough to carry a galvanized iron bucket and strong-stomached enough to muck out, could get work at the Zoo. Farm labourers and good stockmen alike had traded in their jobs with sheep and cows, for antelope and elephants. The Zoo was, in no way, the scientific establishment it is today.

So, with the car park laid out, Restaurant, Cloisters and five refreshment kiosks all staffed by waitresses in white caps and aprons, the Park was ready to cater for its visitors. Extra waitresses were employed for the summer season, living in two converted army huts in the village, where each girl had her own private cubicle. There was hot and cold water and bathrooms, a luxury she probably didn't have in her own home in the early thirties. Small wonder some came back year after year until the Second World War.

On Thursday the twenty-first of May 1931 a special Press Day was held to publicise the opening. It was almost the Whit weekend. Timing was vital. Reports must be in the nation's newspapers by Friday, so that people would know of the opening of this first Country Zoo and plan their weekend visit. Fleet Street's reporters arrived at Luton Station where they were met by special coach and taken to the Zoo for lunch. After lunch they were divided into small groups to be shown round the park. Joan Proctor, who, in spite of her constant ill-health, had been beavering away at all the arrangements for the day, gave herself the largest party to deal with. She loved Whipsnade passionately, especially as it was in what she felt was her part of the country, her paternal grandfather having lived at the Hoo, Great Gaddesden. She was determined that it was going to be given a good press and consequently a good start in life. The reporters departed to flood the nation's newspapers, next day, with the Whipsnade story.

Friday was a special private viewing day for the notables of the area. The County Councils of the three immediate shires, Beds. Bucks. and Herts., were invited together with their Lord Lieutenants and High Sheriffs. Mayors of the local Boroughs came with their Corporations. Everyone was allowed to bring one friend, the Fellows of the Society two. Tea was served to the principal guests and all went away impressed, despite the dull weather and fitful rain which continued over the weekend.

On Saturday May 23rd, the first day that the Park was opened to the general public, one thousand and eighty visitors braved the rain. Sunday's weather was slightly better and some ten thousand came, but the Gods smiled, Bank Holiday Monday dawned fine and sunny and Whipsnade was inundated with visitors. The immediate and immensely popular effect it would have had been completely under-estimated as had the power of the press to advertise. The 'world and his wife' converged on the Park.

The approach roads were not ready for the sudden onslaught of motorised traffic. They were leafy, high-banked lanes where people walked and farm carts lumbered on their way to sleepy fields. The fastest thing that most of them had seen, until now, was a trotting pony, prancing high as it pulled a light trap. Recently, the odd car and a lorry or two and the occasional bus, but nothing like the traffic attempting to make its way to Whipsnade on that first Bank Holiday Monday. By

By midday the peaceful countryside was choked with exhaust fumes.   /DG

midday, the peaceful countryside was choked with exhaust fumes and steam as engines overheated in the endless queue. Women fainted, fretful children cried, all pandemonium was let loose as the entire Bedfordshire Constabulary attempted, in vain, to bring some order out of the increasing chaos. They'd never previously encountered a traffic jam of such proportions. A frantic phone call to the Railway Company in London halted train excursions but did little to relieve the situation. The four turnstiles turned relentlessly as some twenty-seven thousand poured into the Park that day. Once through the turnstiles, the visitors, then as now, had a choice of two directions, but how different the landscape was then. Ahead, Duke's Avenue ran like a silver ribbon through a forest, Ivinghoe Gap, the light at the end of the tunnel, varying in hue with the sky from palest blue to fiery sunset red. Before the trees were felled and the undergrowth cleared to make the Elephant paddock and the Chimpanzee House, Whipsnade Wood, to the left of the Avenue, fringed with graceful larches, was thick with oak and ash, extending to the young beeches in Bluebell Wood. The trees sheltered thickets of rhododendron, bracken and foxgloves, where pheasants, startled by approaching visitors along the tiny paths, scurried for shelter. To the right of Duke's Avenue, behind the cottage where I lived, where the old wood has been replaced by the cheetah enclosures, rose tall straight pine trees – a pack of wolves slinking, sinisterly, between their trunks. Howling eerily at the slightest disturbance, be it a car back-firing, the five o'clock hooter sounding for the works staff to knock off, or the wind moaning through the branches above them. As a child, I would lie awake on winter nights hoping that wind would be strong enough to bring down one of the pines or firs. For the top, or one of the branches, was often my only hope of a Christmas tree. Never once, did I think, as I heard a great tree crashing down, that it might break the fence and set the wolves free.

Such was the magic of Duke's Avenue and, named as it was after the President, the Duke of Bedford, it never occurred to me that it was Central Avenue that was the main road of the Park. Now, with the then undeveloped acres fully in use, I can understand, for it bisects the place as it runs from the Main Gate to Cut Throat Avenue. Neither did it seem much of an Avenue to a small child who'd been told that Avenues were roads lined with trees. True, it had the Bird Sanctuary to its left and part of Whipsnade Wood edged it near the Main Gate, but there were no trees on the Elephant Lawn. I felt that Central Avenue was a bit of a cheat and didn't like it much. But how the years changed my mind! Small trees were planted on both sides which grew into the most graceful Japanese Cherries, fringing the Avenue with clouds of white fragile blossom in the Spring. With foresight other trees were planted between them and, now that the white blossom trees have all died, the Avenue is a great swirl of deepest pink, as though the sunset has been caught in the branches.

Those visitors who chose to start at Duke's Avenue would have passed the wolves in their Pine Wood, the bears in their pit, reached Ouseley Pond and Ouseley Kiosk, gazed with admiration at the pastoral view beyond the Downs and with surprise at the great American bison – a gift from the Duke – in their paddock on the side of the hill. Huge heads with great thick brown fur on their shoulders and comparatively slender hips, like old men ruminating.

The Cherry trees in Central Avenue (circa 1951).   /GS

Those who chose to start in Central Avenue were able to go into Wood Lawn Bird Sanctuary, (which is now hidden by the Ladies and Gents Lavatories), where Keeper Billet offered guided tours. Wood Lawn, the little isolated wood, had been enclosed to make a sanctuary for British wild birds, but one or two foreign ones had crept in. For example, there were Lady Amherst pheasants, the beautifully coloured birds from East China and Tibet, who look for all the world like judges in their wigs, and the Australian brush turkey. This insignificant bird, about the size of a large partridge, or small American turkey, has very big feet with enormous claws and a great hind toe on each foot. It uses these strong feet to build a mound for its eggs during the breeding season. It was fascinating to hide quietly and watch the bird, with its back towards the mound, scratching up earth, leaves and other vegetation behind itself. When the mound was completed – on one occasion in 1934, Keeper Billet recorded one reaching four-and-a-half feet in height, forty-four feet in circumference and weighing almost five tons – the eggs were buried in it and left to hatch. When the young hatch out and wriggle out of the mound, they are fully fledged and able to fly immediately. Brush turkeys roost in trees and feed on grubs and shoots, etc. Another sight in the Bird Sanctuary, in later years, was a huge communal parakeet nest hanging from a tree.

The Australian brush-turkey. /WSB

Beyond the Restaurant and the Water Garden, Whipsnade was already breeding for survival, with a small herd of the almost extinct white Chartley cattle. Wild cattle had roamed freely in Britain until just after Norman times. William the Conqueror had given lands to one Baron de Ferrers in Staffordshire. Under the Charter granted by Henry III the Baron's descendants enclosed their lands, calling the enclosure Chartley Park and driving herds of wild cattle into it. The white animals, larger than other breeds of wild cattle, with black ears and muzzles and long widespreading horns, became known as Chartley cattle. They stayed with the Ferrers family for some seven hundred years, till the beginning of this century, when they were sold and began a series of ups and downs in their fortunes which were to last for the next sixty-five years or so. Fortunately, however, some of the Chartley cattle found their way into the hands of the Duke of Bedford, the great preservationist, and he established a herd at Woburn. He, in turn,

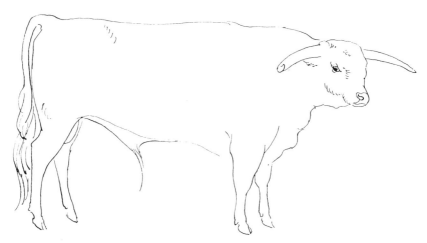

A Chartley bull. During the 1930s the artist John Skeaping decorated the Restaurant walls with animals in this 'cave-like' style. /JS

presented a small herd to Whipsnade, for its opening, along with many other animals, including some Przewalski's Mongolian Wild horses, which he had also saved from extinction, a number of wallabies, Chinese water deer, muntjacs, hog deer and North American turkeys.

Przewalski's Mongolian wild horses which had been saved from extinction by the 11th Duke of Bedford. /BP

The Mongolian wild horses, small animals, barely fourteen hands high, with smooth silken skins, pale faces, dark upstanding manes and little ears, are said to to be the only surviving true wild horse. These little horses shared Dagnall Paddock with the yak – another native of the 'roof of the World'. Yaks are as ungainly as the wild horses are graceful, being humped oxen with long shaggy blackish-brown coats and smooth curved horns.

As yet, there were only three lion cubs, in a pen near the Restaurant. A lion pit was to be made on the side of the Downs. There were several large chalk pits on the downside where, for generations, flints and chalk for road-making had been dug out. Sir Peter intended these eventually to be transformed into enclosures for the large carnivores. Three ancient ones, which were by now grown over with grass, had been fenced in and were occupied by wombats, marmots (Prairie dogs) and woodchuck, small American rodents, similar to marmots but hibernating in winter in a burrow or hollow tree, which they had lined with moss, grass, or dried leaves.

There were lion cubs in a pen near the Restaurant.   */LM*

Above their pits was the Terminus Circle for the bus shuttle which ran from Central Avenue, via Cut Throat Avenue, across Escarpment Avenue, which skirted the top of the Downs and back again, always omitting Duke's Avenue. For a daily ticket, visitors were allowed to get on and off as many times as they liked, at the many stops around the Park. No cars were allowed into the Park in the early days. When they were finally let in, it was, for very many years, on Mondays only.

On the Downs was a single polar bear in a temporary earthen pen complete with pool. It was intended that, eventually, the polar bear would be moved nearer to the other bears by Lady Yule's Walk and Ouseley Pond. This pond was now reached along a narrow gravel path, through a wicket gate. On the northern edge two flights of curved stone steps led to the top of the grass covered reservoir where water pumped from the deep well was stored. Creepers trailed down the balustrades at the side of the steps and over the curved wooden seat placed between them. It was, for me, an entrance to an enchanted castle towering above the little pool. Ouseley, or Coppice Pond, as it has also been called, on whose banks it will be remembered the Council of the Society had made its historic decision to purchase the Whipsnade Estate, was once the local watering place for sheep and horses. When the Society fenced it in, it was obliged to provide a water trough by the roadside which had to be kept constantly filled. As children, we were told that Ouseley Pond never dried up. According to Owen Chamberlain, it was very short of water, a mere puddle, in 1976. In the drought of 1989, however, imagine my horrified thoughts as I gazed in disbelief, at the bottom of the legendary bottomless pool. The mud-baked surface scarred with great cracks, and by November it was overgrown with nettles. But, happily, Sir Peter never saw his fairy pond dried out. He knew it always as it was on the opening day of long ago, freshly planted with flags and other water plants around its verges. Willows trailing their green fingers in its cool clear water. Hazel catkins spilling their heavy, sickly, pollen on its primrose covered banks. Alive with frogs and toads, breeding in their new-found Whipsnade paradise, lizards sliding through its grassy edges. Nearby, peacocks strutted from the shadows and, once bathed in sunlight, spread their fantastic tail feathers, raucously commanding the attention of their dowdy hens and visitors alike. One delighted little boy told his mother that while he watched them 'the peacocks came into bloom'. An apt description for the exquisite beauty of 'the watchmen with a thousand eyes'.

The long day drew to a close. Visitors wound their homeward way, across the lawns to the exit gate. Peter's twenty-year-old dream was, at last, a reality. That evening he and Joan and those who had backed him had every reason to be justly proud.

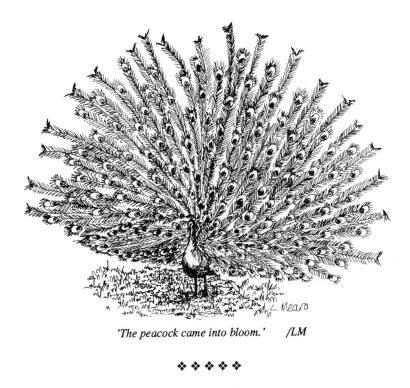

'The peacock came into bloom.'   /LM

❖ ❖ ❖ ❖ ❖

Gradually, Whipsnade's first season drifted towards Autumn and with it Joan Proctor's fragile grasp on life slipped from her fingers. She died in her sleep, on the last day of that golden summer, six weeks after her thirty-fourth birthday. A numbed Whipsnade mourned. No more would the slight, smiling figure be seen riding her pony, Tishy, beside the hawthorn hedge that separated Spicer's Field from Hall Craft and Lay Meadow. They called the narrow path 'Miss Joan's Ride', and Sir Peter, grieving for his young friend and staunchest of allies, forced himself to turn his mind to the very necessary search for large carnivores.

CHAPTER 3

Bostocks and Beyond
(early thirties)

He found the big cats in his native Scotland. The famous, Glasgow-based 'Bostock & Wombwell's Circus & Menagerie' was closing down after one hundred and twenty six years on the road. It had travelled the length and breadth of the British Isles and crossed the seas, carrying its strange and wonderful sights to towns and villages.

Wild animals were rarely seen when zoos were few and far between. Neither were there any of the superb television nature programmes ... There were no televisions ... Occasionally, wild animals crossed the flickering cinema screen, but, for the most part, with a jerky gait, nothing resembling their graceful real life carriage. They were never seen in colour and the colours of the animal kingdom are, surely, the most wonderful sight to behold.

So, in those days, when entertainments were rare, the arrival of the Circus was a red-letter day. Great was the excitement at the sight of its strange and wonderful beasts. Laughter at the antics of the chimpanzees, wonder at the big cats, with thick tawny manes, staring solemnly from behind thick iron bars. Fear, as their tawny eyes gleamed and they bared ferocious teeth and gave out bloodcurdling snarls and roars if anyone dared to go too close to their cages.

The pitching of the Big Top was a spectacle itself as the great weight of canvas rose up and was anchored by thick rope guys attached to huge iron or wooden pegs driven well into the ground. With everything ready, the time of the performance drew near and the excitable queueing for admission began amidst the smell and noise of restless animals waiting to perform. Once inside the Big Top, the crowd jostled for places on the narrow wooden seats that surrounded the surprisingly small sawdust ring. Suddenly, a roll of drums heralded the suave Ring Master, superbly dressed, complete with shiny black top hat. In the hushed expectancy, he announced without the aid of a microphone, that all was ready to begin.

High stepping ponies trotted into the ring – ostrich plumes tossing on their nodding, well-groomed heads. As the music changed, they broke into a fast canter, their riders in glittery sparkling costumes standing on their backs. Great, lumbering, painted elephants, with bejewelled head-dresses, danced in time to lively music – balanced on one leg – stood with all four feet on the surface of upturned wooden tubs – stepped carefully over a crate of eggs or their trainer lying on the sawdust-covered floor. Raised their trunks in salute, trumpeted 'good-bye', and ran from the ring, their large bottoms and little tails wobbling. The cacophony as the clowns came tumbling in with buckets of water and custard pies. The sad, white-faced clown in his beautiful silken costume. The clumsy, shuffling, bewigged, bulbous-nosed Augustes, up to their dirty tricks. They fooled around the edge of the ring, up and down between the rows of onlookers, keeping the audience amused, while in the centre of the ring a great iron cage was dexterously erected for the dangerous acts. The clowns gone, now they came: lumbering bears; great cats – striped tigers or tawny lions – slinking through the steel-barred tunnel from the confinement of their small cages to stretch their legs and flex their muscles in the large cage in the arena. A trainer accompanying them, with no more protection than a whip. The faint-hearted in the audience hid their eyes. Hearts thumped ... Adrenalin flowed ... The callous, like their Roman predecessors, longing for the sight of blood. Their acts over, the dangerous beasts were driven back to their vans – the spotlights swung upwards to the roof of the tent and, while the cage was dismantled, the trapeze artistes entertained. All too soon, the lights swung back to the ring, for the finalé. The Grand Parade of animals that had performed and from the menagerie, clowns and tumblers acrobats and jugglers. The crowd, moving from their seats, suddenly realising how stiff they were; how silent the deserted ring ... happy and tired ... home to bed. But, only too fitful to sleep, for it would be a night filled with the strange sounds of the circus and its creatures.

Again, all too soon, the Big Top would come down and the Circus wend its way to pitch in another place to delight other people. But, for 'Bostocks', the Big Top had come down for the last time. The gaily coloured vans went, not to a new venue, but rolled sadly back to base. The end had come for the era of its Circus days. But, for one hundred and fifty of its birds and animals, a new life lay ahead – a life in the green fields and grassy uplands of the Chiltern Hills.

On a mid-January morning in 1932, Frank Bostock, muffled against the chill Scottish air, watched the bright yellow cages being loaded for departure. They were securely chained to flat railway wagons, and his animals started off on what, for most of them, would be the last journey of their hitherto nomadic lives. As they went on their way, he promised himself that he would visit Whipsnade later in the year to see how they had all settled in.

The train stopped at Carlisle for the animals to be fed. A newspaperman reported that fourteen pounds of meat was thrown to each of the twelve lions. Word spread like wildfire throughout the town. Sightseers swamped the station. For the price of a penny platform ticket, over seven hundred people seized the chance to see the animals. The police were forced to lock the station gates for fear of the crush. Children cheered as, finally, the 'Noah's Ark' train steamed on its way.

Next stop was Lancaster in the early hours of the following morning. The unsuspecting townsfolk suddenly found themselves awakened by terrifying noises. Hyaenas and wolves howling ... Lions roaring ... Elephants trumpeting ... The two Indian elephants – Rosie and Dixie – were, for some reason, unnaturally disturbed by the events of the night; so much so, that their trainer, George Braham, bedded himself down with them. Forty minutes later, the train made off again, leaving Lancaster to settle back to sleep. Just before ten o'clock the train drew into Dunstable North station, where Captain Beal, together with several of his keepers, was waiting to welcome his new animals and accompany them on the last leg of their four hundred mile journey.

The people of Dunstable hadn't expected to see vivid yellow Circus vans hauled through their streets by railway tractors on that grey January day. They stood and stared as elephants and dromedaries were led along the road towards the Downs, the animals, no doubt, glad to stretch their legs again. After almost two hours, the strange procession arrived at the Zoo Main Gate, open awaiting their arrival. I watched, wide-eyed, as it passed through.

Once inside the safety of the park, the elegantly beautiful cranes were released beneath woodland trees as graceful as the birds themselves. The red 'Boxing' kangaroo was turned loose. The dromedaries were led away to a prepared paddock. The polar bear was introduced to the one already in its enclosure on the Downs. Rosie and Dixie, never separated in all their circus lives together, were parted. Rosie was led away to join Nurjar Khan, the Indian elephant already resident at Whipsnade. Dixie made to follow her friend, but was drawn back and chained to a tree. Captain Beal said she wouldn't be staying.

End of line for menagerie

The Bostock Animals leaving Dunstable North Station, January 1932. Captain Beal is on the far right in a trilby hat with Hugh Simmons, the Clerk of the Works, beside him. The camel on the left is led by Bert Matthews, the other by Frank Meakins. The hatless young man in the centre, Basil Simmons, was in later years to take charge of the Pheasantry. Rosie and Dixie bring up the rear. /DG

'If you want a fine, friendly, willing, good-tempered elephant, as careful not to hurt a puny man as you would be not to hurt a baby, you can have Dixie for £500', he announced. Deeply distressed, unable to understand why she'd been separated from her friend, Dixie stood morosely throwing earth over her head. Her beloved trainer, George Braham, sought to console her. Choked himself, he crossed to the solitary animal and, softly whispering in her ear, comforted her as best he could. Gently, she wound her trunk affectionately round his waist. In this alien and unfriendly place, he was all she had left. She held on to him as long as she could.

Meanwhile, the men were endeavouring to move the fifty foot wagons into a close knit semi-circle so that they could be covered by a marquee to give them some protection from the weather. Even with the aid of a tractor, they couldn't manage to manoeuvre them. What was second nature to a circus team, was proving a seemingly insoluble problem for keepers and works' staff alike. Until someone thought of the solitary elephant. Untethering her, George led Dixie across to the wagons and, with a word of encouragement, demonstrated what it was he wanted her to do. Lowering her huge head, she pushed against the first wagon and, as the army of men guided it, rolled it into place.

So the afternoon proceeded, with Dixie completely happy now that she was busy, pushing while the men positioned, stopping, now and again, to tackle biscuits and apples proffered by admiring bystanders. It was just like being back in the circus again. For a while, Rosie was forgotten. Dixie's huge face seemed to be wreathed in smiles! As their day of arrival drew to its close, the animals who were still in cages and Dixie, who was waiting to be deported, found themselves once more gathered together under a large tent. With the familiar flapping of the canvas in her ears, a tired and contented Dixie nodded off to sleep. I don't know if it was that first afternoon's work that won Captain Beal over, or what exactly made the powers-that-be change their minds, but, in the end, it was Rosie who went to Bristol. Dixie stayed. Stayed to delight visitors and staff alike, young and old, down the long years until her death in 1963. But, over the next few months, her talents were put to good use moving logs and helping to lay electricity cables.

Dixie's strength was again put to good use when it came to laying the electricity cable to the kiosks. My father is in the centre of this very old picture with his hand on the drum. George Braham is at Dixie's head. /JD

Meanwhile, workmen were busy on the Downs, erecting strong iron bars round one of the larger chalk pits to make the lions' den. The sloping banks of the chalk pit had grown over with grass and scrub.

Small caves were dug into the bankside to provide shelter and part of the steeper, southern side of the pit was to be a concrete wall some seventeen feet high. At the top there would be a lowish barrier so that the panoramic view of the lions in their dell would be unobstructed.

There had been two setbacks with the concreting programme. The first had been delay due to severe frost in February. The second was the crumbling effect the chalk had on the concrete. There hadn't been too many problems when making a similar wall at the Bear pit in Lady Yule's Walk, but now they were actually working on the chalk face. Eventually it was decided that reinforced concrete would have to be used.

These delays meant that, to Sir Peter's disappointment, the Bostock lions were still in their circus wagons at Easter and during these months they had foregone the exercise they were used to in the circus ring. By the time the pit was ready, it was decided that Cecil – a lion so ferocious that he had already killed another lion – would be safer in a cage in the London Zoo than being let out with the others.

However, once the concrete problem was solved successfully, it led to two more projects farther along the Downs escarpment. By now the two huge polar bears had so churned up the mud in their enclosure it was cemented throughout, including the making of a large cave with a concrete ledge for them to sleep on. The tiger pit was all concrete too. It was dug to a depth of some twenty feet. A concrete hill was constructed in the middle of it, rising up from the side of the pond with terraced sides, like a very small version of the Mappin Terraces. The lower part of the eastern curve of this circular pit was terraced as well, in order to give the tigers a variety of levels for exercise. A felled tree trunk was dragged in and flung horizontally across the bottom of the pit for them to scratch their claws on. No doubt, both of these 'Christmas cake' looking constructions were easy for the keepers to keep clean, but they always seemed to me to belong more to Regent's Park than Whipsnade.

Work also started on cutting out a chalk lion on the Downs, based on the white horses at Westbury in Wiltshire and near Uffington Castle in Berkshire and the Giants at Cerne Abbas in Dorset and Wilmington in Sussex. The Old Man of Wilmington is two hundred and twenty-six feet tall – the Whipsnade Lion was to be four hundred and eighty feet long, the tail width thirteen feet and its total perimeter three-eighths of a mile. This now famous landmark was no mean undertaking. Not only was there the physical effort of cutting and digging – there was the piling up of chalk as well, since this lion is not an outline but a solid shape with its head some six feet in depth. All this, manually, with pick and shovel. It was necessary to make frequent visits across to Ivinghoe Beacon to check the accuracy of the shape. Designed by R B Brook-Greaves, the chalk lion took about eighteen months to make and, in spite of blizzards in March, Sir Peter had his largest lion of all by Easter 1933.

A pit for the tigers was dug out of the chalk face of the Downs. After the war Kodiak bears were exhibited in the pit. It has now been infilled. /JD

By July, the tigers Tom and Ranee had produced their first litter of three cubs, who, amid great excitement, were put on show to the public in August, when they were six weeks old. Tom and Ranee produced many litters down the years until Tom drowned himself in their drinking pool, in only eighteen inches of water. He was succeeded by a sturdy man-eater who had killed four natives while he was being captured.

Tom and Ranee's first litter would need a den of their own by the following year. The tiger pit was not large enough to house five full-grown tigers, so two old chalk pits near Holly Frindle were fenced off and a pond made. This dell, overgrown with bushes and scrub, was

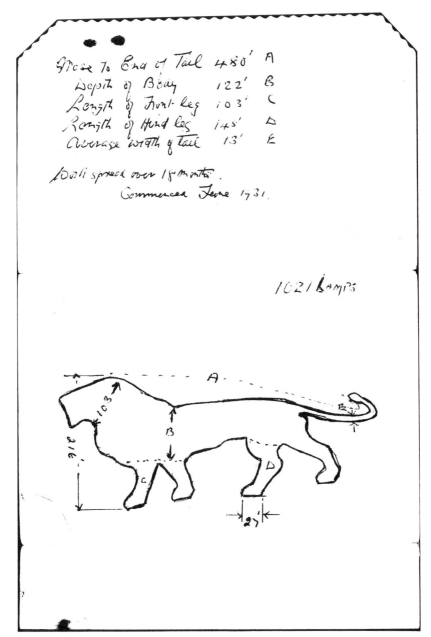

My father's plan of the Chalk Lion which he later used when planning the lighting for the first time for the Park's 21st Birthday.

Ranee with her three cubs. They were the first tiger cubs to be born to the Zoological Society for fifty years. Tigers have bred well at Whipsnade ever since.   /BP

a far more natural home than the barren concrete pit. At first, it was though it would only be suitable during the summer months and they would need to winter in the indoor quarters adjacent to the pit. But, Sir Peter pointed out that tigers had migrated from the cold Asiatic highlands. They would still be able to thrive amid frost and snow, provided they had adequate shelter from the wind and a good diet. It is unusual and delightful to see the beautiful, colourful creatures cavorting in the snow.

On the other side of Escarpment Avenue from all this activity lay the peaceful expanse of Spicers, a field as large as the whole of the London Zoo. To this field, Percy and Jean, the first pygmy hippos to have bred in captivity, came for the summer holidays. Sir Peter had always hoped that Whipsnade would serve as a holiday home and recuperating resort for the London animals. The pygmy hippos were regular summer visitors in my childhood years. I always felt that summer had begun when the smart London Zoo lorry

I always felt summer had begun when the pygmy hippos came down from London for their holidays.   /BP

38

swung through the Main Gate on one of its twice-weekly runs with the pygmy hippos in the crates on board. Once let loose in Spicers, they stretched their short little legs and gambolled around the big field, swam in the pool and grew fat, cropping the luscious clover. Tortoises came for their summer holidays too, giant tortoises, big enough for me to sit on.

By now Nurjar and Dixie had established the hoped-for riding service. Two sets of double wooden steps had been built and positioned, with a gap between them just wide enough for an elephant to pass through. Passengers climbed up the steps and were strapped into the seats of the houdah, three or four to a side, back to back. The elephant walked away from the steps along the Elephant Walk to its terminus circle, where she re-traced her journey back to the steps for the passengers to disembark at the end of the three-penny ride.

Nurjar was sedate, as befitted someone whose name meant 'Indian Princess'! She gave a solid, steady ride, her keepers walking either side of her, a solemn expression on her long face. Dixie, on the other hand, gave a joyous, boisterous, wobbly ride as she swayed to remembered music, the dark, dapper George, who had come from the circus with her, sitting on her neck – white teeth gleaming beneath his waxed moustache, knees pressed behind his ears to direct her. Not that Dixie needed directing. She knew the way alone. In the same way that she would have shown loving care for her passengers, with or without her

In the centre of the picture keepers are sweeping up the elephants' dung and putting it into a dustbin, a regular feature of a busy afternoon. I have never tasted tomatoes as sweet as those my father grew in his days at the Park when he fertilised them with elephant manure. /DG

keeper's presence. It was, for me, a wonderful sight to see her lifting George up onto her neck. Curling her trunk round his waist, she swung him up as easily as if he had been a rag doll and always there was a smile on her seemingly round face. In fact, the smile on her face only faded when, retired from riding in 1962, she had nothing to do. She became a film star, or rather a film 'extra', being taken regularly to the studios to appear in the 1930s' version of the film 'Elephant Boy', with Sabu. I was very indignant that 'our Dixie' didn't play the lead. She kept up her circus tricks too. On winter mornings, after the elephants' exercise walk round the main roads of the Park was over, she could be seen balancing on an upturned tub, or sitting on a park bench, then wondering why it collapsed, not understanding that it wasn't reinforced like her circus seat. And she played the mouth organ! A 'skill' which the other elephants soon acquired!

Before I started school the keepers led the Shetland ponies, and I am pictured with Alf Bransom. The stirrups were adjusted to a standard length and I can still recall the thrill when my legs were at last long enough to reach them.

Nurjar and Dixie were joined by two baby elephants during May 1932. These two little elephants, standing no more than five feet at the shoulder, were gifts from Mr Alfred Ezra. They were some three years old and were called Mangal Peary (Best Beloved) and Bhisca Peary (Beloved Beggar). Before the present elephant house was built, Dixie and the two babies shared a house, Nurjar living on her own. So it wasn't surprising the little ones soon picked up some of Dixie's tricks, including playing the mouth organ. Though, to be fair, blowing through her trunk into the small instrument was something even the more serious minded Nurjar later learned, as well.

The sonorous sounds, emanating from the elephant house, were all part of the summer symphony of Whipsnade long ago, the staccato click of the turnstiles, the chattering of monkeys, the deep-throated roar of distant lions, the shrill, sharp cry of the peacock, the two-toned moan of the gibbons. These were the sounds that greeted me as, hurrying home from school, I ran straight to the Elephant Lawn for my rides. Since mine were free, I seldom had them on a Saturday and

The camel riding circle was originally near the Round Close fence. The first rides were very rocky and one sat on a saddle fastened to the Arabian camel's one hump. This animal was replaced by two-humped Bactrian camels, which were able to carry one passenger on their necks and one large or two small between the humps and felt a much safer ride. Albert Cole leads the camel, Frank Meakins the middle pony and Alf Bransom the front one. Alf's sister Flossie was in charge of the Linen Room at the Restaurant and his brother Arthur was my father's assistant. Arthur sustained one of the first accidents in the Park by losing some fingers while attending to the pump.   /DG never on Sundays or Bank Holidays. There was no riding, pre-war, on Mr MacDonald's day off (Fridays), reckoned to be the quietest day of the week, so there was a certain urgency on Mondays, Tuesdays, Wednesdays and Thursdays.

Rae Walker led the Shetland pony. She was the first woman on the menagerie staff, later being joined by Kitty Keen. Kitty sometimes helped out with the bears, but, in the main, they were employed to be pony girls – mucking out the stables, feeding and grooming the smart little black animals, and leading them up and down the lawn for the children to ride all afternoon. Keepering was very much a male only prerogative in those days.

Albert Cole and Alf Bransom took it in turns to lead the camels. Alf was a village boy who had, like so many, found work at the Zoo. Albert Cole had come to Whipsnade with animals from Sir Anthony Wingfield's private collection at Ampthill. He was a big man always impeccably turned out – I can still see the shine on his black leather gaiters as I write – as I can still feel the warmth and softness of the camel's hair as I sank between the humps, or sat on its big strong neck, my arms entwined around it. It was a gentle swaying plod like the ride on Nurjar Khan.

CHAPTER 4

The Golden Years – My Africa
(thirties continued)

In July 1932, the *Daily Mirror* reported that 'a strange unwanted creature had invaded the sylvan beauties of Whipsnade Zoo'. Everyone in the Park knew all too well about this creature.

The Park was plagued by rabbits. They flourished on the Downs, burrowing into the chalky soil. Angus Macdonald, the first head keeper and later first Overseer, did his best to reduce them, going out daily with his gun and his black spaniel, Pam. One year two thousand eight hundred rabbits were reported killed and some one thousand five hundred were sent to the London Zoo. Apart from those fed to the carnivores, many others found their way to the dinner tables of the Whipsnade staff and were a grateful supplement to the meagre meat ration during World War II.

But the creature the *Mirror* wrote about could not be dispatched by Angus Macdonald and his gun. It was with the zoo for many, many years. It was 'homo vulgaris' – the litter lout. Naïvely optimistic, Sir Peter had requested through the pages of the first Guide Book, that visitors should treat the Park with the same respect they would show a private garden. Initially, he was able to report that they had responded well. But, of course, it didn't last. By the end of a busy day the place was awash with litter. Every morning a group of paper pickers emerged from the Works' Yard, well before opening time. On Mondays and Tuesdays after Bank Holidays their ranks were swelled by every available keeper and member of the Works' department who could be spared. Armed with sacks and spiked sticks they swept through the Park in an endeavour to have it clean and tidy by 10 a.m. In an attempt to keep on top of things, Scouts and Rovers from a local Troop eventually came in on Sundays to pick up some of the litter as it was dropped. It is only now, at the time of writing, when we seem to accept rubbish and graffiti as the norm, that the Zoo is virtually trouble free. Owen Chamberlain says fewer paper pickers spend less hours than at almost any other time in the Park's history. The worst offenders nowadays are squirrels and marauding birds, scavenging through the bins, pulling out rubbish in their search for tasty morsels and scattering it on the ground.

But dumping litter wasn't the only misdeed of the general public. One fine Spring afternoon, they ravaged 'Clappers' or 'Bluebell Wood' as it was now called. An irate keeper arrived at the office. So many visitors were picking bluebells, they couldn't stop them, he reported breathlessly. Leaving his desk, Captain Beal marched to the Main Gate. Commandeering all the available litter baskets, he ordered them to be positioned either side of the Main Gate, and the Exit turnstile to be shut off. He waited, flanked by the Park Policeman and the Overseer, both looking most formidable in their dark uniforms. I often climbed up to my bedroom window to watch the crowds going home; on that particular day I wondered who Captain Beal was waiting for. Before long I knew, as the unsuspecting hordes bore down on the Exit – from Central Avenue, from Duke's Avenue, from the little paths that traversed Whipsnade Wood. All carrying armfuls of bluebells! Whichever way they came there was only one way out, they had to run the gauntlet, past the imposing figure of Captain William Beal. In his deep, commanding voice, he told them, in no uncertain terms, that they were illegally in possession of Zoological Society property and they would not be allowed to remove that property from the Society's premises. They would deposit it in the baskets provided before departing through the gate. I watched sadly as the pretty little flowers were dumped ignominiously in the bins, knowing only too well that, even if we rescued them they wouldn't last. Wild flowers live but a little while once plucked. That evening my parents took me up to Bluebell Wood. Fragmented patches of hyacinth blue which had escaped the greedy fingers lay dotted here and there among the slender trunks of the beech trees where, but a few hours before, a thick, perfumed carpet had covered the whole glade. It took a long time for there to be abundant growth in the wood again, but the Captain's harsh remedy worked. Flowers were never again plundered to anything like the same extent.

Another plundering creature found its way into the Park. This one was more sinister and came in over the boundary fence, at dead of night. It came seeking succulent geese and delectable duck for its dinner. Sometimes the meals for the preying fox set the Society back as much as two hundred pounds each. In a vain attempt to protect the unsuspecting birds, hurricane lamps were set round their living areas. But light did not deter the hungry Renard. At length, it was concluded, the only remedy was to change the overhang on the boundary fence so that it curved outwards. Originally, the inward curving overhang had been added to the high perimeter fence to allay the fears of local villagers by showing them that everything possible was being done to keep the wild animals in. Even so, suspicious farm labourers, passing on their way to work, had been seen prodding the sturdy fence, to make sure it was secure and, at least one farmer was known to keep a gun by his bed. After some deliberation, the overhang was reversed and barbed wire was added. The problem of foxes entering was solved.

As for the inmates escaping, considering the numbers that have lived in the Park down the years, remarkably few have escaped and the most serious pre-war accident was caused, not by an animal getting out, but by a human being getting into one of the enclosures. Most accidents are caused by misjudgement, carelessness, or sheer bravado. Phil Bates had misjudged the porcupines. By now, the young man who had been so gifted at caring for the farmers' sick animals and the villagers' pets was

a fully-fledged Zoo Keeper. But he'd misjudged the porcupines, thinking them to be docile animals, as indeed he had found them to be, until one morning when he was cleaning them out four males hurtled themselves at him for no apparent reason, jabbing him in the legs with their long sharp quills. Despite bleeding profusely from the lacera-tions, he managed to beat

Phil Bates misjudged the porcupine .   /BP

them off with a broom and make his escape.

Another accident, as he admitted himself, was caused by simple forget-fulness. He and his assistant were putting the feed into the bison paddock when, to their horror, they saw the bison trooping out. Too late, they realised they hadn't shut the gate properly. Swiftly following the animals and shouting and waving their pitchforks, they managed to round them up like cattle and herd them back into the pen. All save one – a gigantic bull.

Stealthily, still armed with their pitchforks, they crept up behind him. Sensing their presence, the huge creature swung round, lowered his head and charged. Turning, they ran off as fast as their legs would carry them, but Phil's companion, tripping on the uneven ground, fell headlong.

Hearing his cry, Phil stopped, and, seeing his assistant sprawling in the grass, stood guard over him, holding up his pitchfork as the great beast bore down on them. Trembling, Phil stood his ground, holding the only protection afforded them, out in front of him. The bison ran straight into the prongs. Startled and stunned by the sudden sharp pain, it turned away shaking its large sore head. Angered, it charged back into the paddock where, incensed by its own pain, it attacked the first fellow bison it chanced upon, ripping the poor unsuspecting creature's stomach open.

A fine herd of American Bison gave its name to the hill. /BP

Other animal deaths caused by fighting that year included a male Grevy's zebra, a nilgai and a Chillingham cow. Besides helping to preserve the Chartley breed of cattle, the Zoological Society had played a positive part in preserving the famous herd of cattle from Chillingham Castle in Northumberland. Due to the heavy cost of maintenance, the herd had been in danger of being broken up in 1931, when the Society came to the rescue. Now, these small cattle, with their short upturned horns and longish curly white hair, although appearing timid are in fact very fierce. If they feel threatened by the approach of a stranger, the herd will gallop away, turn and, walking back half the distance, stop and stare at the interloper. If he makes any movement at all, they will gallop off again, but only for a shorter distance, stop and turn and now walk back closer. Each time they are disturbed, they will repeat this procedure until they are so forebodingly close that the enemy retreats. Their paddock was near the Restaurant. In the early years, the Catering Department was self-catering. Cakes, rolls, etc. were baked in the bakehouse, and patisserie in the main Restaurant complex. These delectable items were ferried round the

MAN KILLED BY LIONS

WHIPSNADE ZOO EMPLOYEE'S FATAL VENTURE

ATTACKED WHILE TRYING TO RECOVER A HAT

THE LATE MR. STANLEY L. STENSON

A newspaper photograph showing where Stanley Stenson climbed into the lion pit.

Park to the various kiosks in the department's own small fleet of vehicles. I can still recall, vividly, the smell of the baking and the mouthwatering sight of these items being loaded into the vans.

Stanley Stenson, a young man of twenty-six from Studham, was a Catering Department driver. One afternoon, in June 1934, for reasons best known to himself, he was down by the lion pit. Surrounded by admiring visitors, the sleek lions, who had recently been fed, were basking contentedly on the grass in the warmth of the afternoon sunshine. As Stanley approached the parapet at the southern end of the pit, a visitor suddenly threw a hat over the barrier. Drawing nearer, Stanley looked down at the hat resting on the concrete at the base of the high parapet wall. 'I'd go in and get that for five hundred

47

quid,' he said to the man. 'Huh! I bet you wouldn't,' a bystander retorted. Immediately, Stanley climbed over the barrier. There was a sloping grassy bank formed by the side of the old chalk pit to his right. This bank was separated from the parapet by a row of bars running at right-angles from the main fence, which served as protection, so that the lions couldn't jump from the bank over the low parapet barrier. No doubt, Stanley meant to use this fence to help him get down to the bottom of the pit and up and out again. After all, the well-fed lions were resting docilely across the other side of their lair!

But things swiftly started going horribly wrong … Stanley slipped. Horace Myhill, the man who'd thrown his hat into the pit, grabbed hold of him. Startled, one of the lions crossed the grass. Leaping up, it seized Stanley's foot. In the ensuing struggle between men and beast, Stanley's boot came off! Then he and Myhill lost their holds! Stanley dropped into the pit, banging his head on the concrete, some seventeen feet below. Screaming and shouting broke out from hitherto stunned and horrified onlookers as the lion dragged Stanley's limp body across the pit floor as easily and playfully as a cat would drag a mouse. Alerted, keepers hurried to the pit, blowing whistles to raise the alarm. Seizing pitchforks and brooms they banged on the bars and the metal sides of the 'catch-up' in an attempt to distract the lion. Someone hurried to the office for Captain Beal and guns. Members of staff working at the new Giraffe house climbed the fence and, ignoring the danger of zebra, raced across Spicers Field to find out what was happening and what help they could offer. Captain Beal arrived with a shotgun. Eventually, the lions were driven into the catch-ups and the body retrieved. Stanley was carried out of the lion pit, shocked visitors and staff standing silently by. His body was put on the back of one of the Zoo's lorries and covered with a tarpaulin.

I had chicken pox at the time and was looking out of my bedroom window when I saw the lorry coming very, very slowly down Duke's Avenue. I wondered what was under the tarpaulin. When my father came in, he told me. He was one of the men who'd run across the zebra field. The tragedy hit the headlines in the nation's newspapers, as it did again at the time of the inquest. Captain Beal was praised for his prompt action. The Society was exonerated from all blame. Nevertheless, precautions were taken immediately after the accident to ensure that nothing like it could ever happen again.

Ironically, lions must, at that time, have been some of the least valuable of the large animals in the Park. Worth a hundred and twenty pounds each in 1920, successful breeding both in this country and on the continent had brought the price down to only five pounds each.

The most valuable animal of the day was the giraffe. I'd seen the giraffes walking sedately in their house and small courtyard at the London Zoo, watched as they splayed their long legs in order to reach

A mother giraffe with her baby. Rosie's baby Boxer was to be born on Boxing Day 1937, Whipsnade's first giraffe calf. /LM

their drinking water and noticed how high their feeding boxes were fixed, near to the top of the wall. I didn't know at that stage that they were the tallest animals in the world - nor that the animals of Africa had been designed for 'lateral feeding'. That means that each species finds food at a certain level and that the giraffe feeds off the topmost branches of the trees - eating leaves and twigs even above the height the elephant is able to reach. Nor did I know they could move swiftly. Now, they were coming to Whipsnade. A big house had been built and a large area of grass in front of it enclosed by a sturdy fence. There was great excitement when the new arrival came. I stood looking up at Rosie, the gracefully tall, pale brown creature, covered with beautifully patterned darker blotches, looking down at us from almost three times the height of Captain Beal. Bert Rogers, her Keeper, opened the gate which led from the courtyard into the paddock. I held my breath as the animal stretched her long legs and stepped daintily onto the grassy paddock then, suddenly realising how much space lay in front of her, she moved swiftly down the field with the strangest movement I had ever seen. She moved, for all the world, like a giant, long-legged, rocking horse.

Nowadays, most of us have seen television pictures of giraffes moving swiftly across the African Savannas, but it is not the same as seeing it in real life. As my older daughter, Rebecca, who was born in Whipsnade Park, says, 'Television doesn't give you the warmth or the smell of the animals'. She is quite sure that if someone blindfolded her and took her into a giraffe house, she would know where she was by the unique odour that has lingered in her memory down the years. But, on that childhood day of mine, so long ago, as I watched the giraffe move down the paddock with its great long strides ... saw zebra grazing in the haze of Spicers Field beyond ... Whipsnade became 'My Africa'.

Much later, in the fifties, when John Huston had finished the location shots for his film 'The African Queen' and had come to London to finish filming in a studio, he realised he lacked a view of zebra in the rain. So he brought his film crew to Whipsnade. Needless to say, it was a fine day, so my father laid out perforated hosepipes across Spicers Field, and, turning on the water, became a 'rain maker'. It's a very brief shot in the film - zebra grazing in the rain - but it convinced me that Whipsnade can, indeed, be a substitute Africa for those of us who have never been fortunate enough to know the real thing, and it makes nonsense of the arguments of some of those who denigrate zoos.

A zebra.   /LM

The new Giraffe House was a break from the original animal sheds, in the same way that the Superintendent's new house had broken with the style of the early houses, which, it will be recalled, had been closely based on the traditional design of Hall Farm. The Superintendent's house had been finished for Captain Beal and his family to move into in January 1932. It was a wooden structure built in the mansard style and made from Colombian pine, except for the front door, staircase and loggia, which were English oak. The Estate offices were incorporated in the ground floor, the Captain's office, where he spent many long evenings poring over his extensive stamp collection, backing onto his sitting room. Beyond were two wooden garages and a third similar structure which was used as a St John's Ambulance Brigade Station. Members of St John's were always on duty at the Park in the early years at least on Sundays and Bank Holidays. The Superintendent's house and the office block had been designed by Sir Albert Richardson, the 'Professor' of Ampthill and later President of the Royal Academy.

The Giraffe House and the new Elephant House were to come from a very different drawing-board. In 1930, a young, Russian born architect, Berthold Lubetkin, had come to Britain. Two years later, together with six newly qualified architects, he formed a group called Tecton. Tecton designed the Giraffe House, which was a very tall narrow building. I assumed it was tall and narrow because that was the shape of giraffes! I had no idea that the Giraffe House, or the new Elephant House, presaged the future. Neither did the grown-ups know just how right they were, when they said the Elephant House, the Lavatory block opposite and the two bungalows at Holly Frindle, all Lubetkin designed in the same style, looked like something out of H G Wells' 'Things to Come'.

The new concrete Elephant House, forerunner of the post-war high rise flats.   /DP

Until 1934, the elephants had lived in two separate wooden buildings where, for safety's sake, they had to be hobbled, and that was why they were taken for a walk round the Park every morning. Now they were to have a brand new house, complete with built-in swimming pool, where they would all four be able to live together. The Elephant House, which is still in use and is now a Grade 2 Listed building, was made from reinforced, fire-proof concrete. A long, low building, it comprised four circular 'huts', each with a circular glass roof and huge, curved, steel sliding doors. In front of the cubicles, stretching the entire length of the building, was the bathing pool – and across the front of each cubicle, to prevent the elephants from falling into the water, was a row of very short spikes – so the animals were still hobbled as protection from the spikes! Later, after one or two nasty falls, the spikes were replaced by iron barriers. Although the new house was to be home to both Nurjar and Dixie until their deaths in comparative old-age, an architectural journal of the 1930s described it as being 'only suitable for young elephants'. Presumably no one told the Zoological Society! It was one of my delights to see the huge animals wallowing in their bath after a busy afternoon giving rides - and watch, with glee, as the elephants sprayed the unsuspecting visitors with water from their trunks!

Across Central Avenue, everyone called the concrete toilet block 'The Russian Lavatories', in deference to the architect. The Zoological Society had employed Tecton to design a new Gorilla House at the London Zoo, as well as the new buildings at Whipsnade. All these structures aroused wide public interest in the group and, in 1935, together with the very futuristic almost sculptured Penguin Pool at Regent's Park, they completed their first building of major importance, a block of flats - Highpoint - at Highgate. This building was also constructed from reinforced concrete and used 'load bearing' walls instead of the more usual independent frame. These flats were very luxurious. I went there once to visit Dr Vevers, the London Zoo's Superintendent. Then, in 1939, Tecton completed a Health Centre for Finsbury, the first British Local Government Authority to become patrons of modern architecture. After the war, Lubetkin and Tecton's ideas were extensively copied. Little did the Whipsnade folk realise in 1934 that their new buildings were the forerunners of post war 'high rise' concrete flats.

Mr Lubetkin had the use of one of the two bungalows at Holly Frindle and Sir Peter based himself in the other one on his many visits to Whipsnade instead of the Secretary's flat at Hall Farm. He loved the privacy of Holly Frindle, having previously had an old London bus converted into a study on a plot of land in the isolated part of the Park where visitors were not allowed to go. This was the Dagnall side of the Park, where he had had such high hopes of a great Main Entrance served by the railway.

In 1935, in his seventy first year, Sir Peter reluctantly decided the time had come to give up his Secretaryship of the Zoological Society. His one regret, he said, was leaving Whipsnade, as he closed the door on his 'Russian' bungalow and set out for a villa in Malaga in Spain. But Sir Peter's sojourn in the sun was to be shortlived. In July 1936 the Spanish Civil War broke out and after many horrifying and heartbreaking experiences, he finally left on HMS Ardent, helping two anti-Fascist Spanish friends to escape, in a cloak and dagger plot, almost emulating the Scarlet Pimpernel. Sir Peter spent the greater part of the rest of his life at Whipsnade, even becoming an ARP Warden during the War. Thus, was I given, by pure chance, the opportunity to know better the giver of my much loved Teddy.

An immediately pre-war map of the Park. /GB(ii)

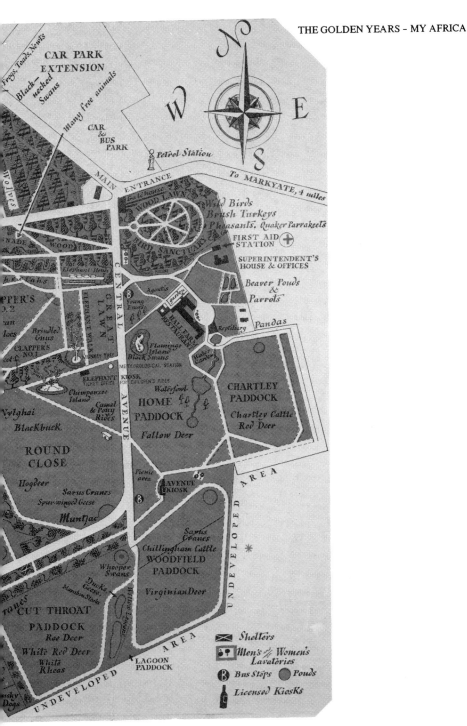

CHAPTER 5

War

The Society's new Secretary was Dr Julian Huxley. Like Sir Peter, he too was a scientist and he wore spectacles, but there, to the sceptical Zoo 'grapevine,' any resemblance between the two men ended. The tall, white-haired Sir Peter had always appeared so dignified, so impeccably dressed, in well-cut tweed suits, or plus fours, his legs encased in unwrinkled socks. Dr Huxley, on the other hand, wore crumpled jackets that hung comfortably about him, his dark brown unruly hair falling over his forehead. He brought an entourage of family and young friends. A wife who spoke with a foreign accent and wore red hats … both of which some local folk, my mother included, found slightly shocking. They all camped in a wooden hut over in Sir Peter's Way and rode Iceland ponies round the Park in casual clothes! Besides, hadn't his younger brother written a book called 'Brave New World', about dreadful scientific things that would happen in the future?! How could anyone think of some of his ideas? Never mind write about them! His grandfather, Thomas Huxley, had coined a new word 'Agnostic', for people who didn't know if they believed in God or not; and hadn't he been a friend of Charles Darwin … the man who said we all came from monkeys?! Misgivings about the new Secretary ran rife. The Huxleys were bohemian, everyone said! For my part, as I grew up, I found Dr Huxley a kind, friendly man, who let me ride his Iceland ponies and camp in the wooden hut with my friend Gill, when his family didn't need it.

But the bohemian image was further fostered by the arrival of artist, John Skeaping, to decorate the Restaurant. Using what looked like a gun, he sprayed pictures of animals … just like prehistoric cave paintings … each one caught for ever in movement, on the Restaurant walls. Though, sadly, the pictures were not to last for ever; they were painted over after the War. Perhaps, after all, it was only the eye of a child that fully appreciated the beauty of John Skeaping's work because the grown-ups didn't think much of his 'Stallion' either.

John Skeaping's 'Stallion'. /ZO

'Stallion', was a huge mahogany sculpture, said to be one of the largest carvings in the world of its day. It was under threat of being broken up and only the head preserved, when a group of Skeaping's admirers subscribed to save it, so 'Stallion' came to Whipsnade in May 1937. He was placed on a brick plinth in the centre of the Ouseley Bus circle, facing across the valley, where he stood, half drawing back, as though startled by something in the view the human eye couldn't see. His wooden eyes bulged, nostrils flared, every muscle in his great mahogany body flexed and rippling in the sunlight. He was the guardian of the Downland scarp of the Park for some ten years. Then, the 'Philistines' who covered up the wall paintings, dismantled his plinth and sent him to languish in the Tate Gallery.

At this time, three islands were constructed in Central Avenue. One for flamingoes, by the Restaurant. The other two for gibbons and chimpanzees, across the road, and an open air reptillary for grass snakes and wall lizards near the cloisters end of the Restaurant. For Billy and Laura Beal, John Macdonald the Overseer's son, and me, it was pure magic to go onto these islands, when the workmen and visitors had gone home, at the end of the day. Although we enjoyed seeing the animals, when they arrived, we felt that we had been robbed of our 'desert islands'.

The Gibbon island was flat. The small apes, acrobats of the S.E. Asian forests, swung their silvery-grey bodies effortlessly from tree to tree, hanging on with their incredibly strong arms, high above our heads, uttering their strange whooping cry. Or they ran to the water's edge, their long arms held high above their heads, staring curiously at the visitors on the other side of the moat, or gazed at their own small faces, reflected in its glimmering surface.

The Chimp island rose to a rocky hill in the centre, under which was a cave-like shelter, where they could be shut in at night. The island had a branched tree trunk for them to climb and a monkey puzzle tree, for embellishment. It was not long before the chimps were to set two popular fallacies to rest. The first was the monkey puzzle tree ... 'Monkeys can't climb it, you see!' everybody said. Perhaps because chimps are apes, they not only climbed all over it, but eventually succeeded in killing it altogether in the process! The other fallacy was that, because chimps couldn't swim, the moat would keep them secure on the island and only a low barrier was needed round the moat to stop visitors falling in! One afternoon, I was selling postcards from a tray, by the chimp island, when, to my surprise, one of them, executing a beautiful crawl stroke, swam smartly across the moat and, with equal

The Chimp Island.   /BP

aplomb, climbed over the barrier and made off in the direction of the Giraffe House.

Very soon afterwards the chimps were taken off the island and sent back to London. Sea-lions, for many years, inhabited the island in their place, but now they have been moved into the Dolphin Pool and seals swim happily there instead. No doubt glad to be safe from the scourges of disease that have swept through the seal population in the North Sea in recent times.

On Easter Day, 1937, the Bactrian camels, who had been part of the first ever exchange with Moscow Zoo, the previous year, gave birth. It was the first baby camel to be born at Whipsnade. Captain Beal named it 'Hallelujah', which, considering the large numbers born subsequently, down the years, proved most appropriate. On Boxing Day, that year, Rosie gave birth to Boxer, the first baby giraffe for Whipsnade and, incidentally, the first for the Zoological Society for twenty-three years. The Mongolian Wild Horse, born in 1937, was despatched to the Munich Zoo. Wooden hospital sheds for sick animals, with concrete floors for added hygiene, were built in the Works yard and, as the threat of War loomed, work started on an Air Raid Shelter for the public.

The sunny September Sunday morning when War was declared, Billy Beal and I were playing marbles on his front doorstep. As a nation, we had hoped, after Munich in 1938, that war with Germany would be averted. The London Zoo was having a new Elephant House built and two of its elephants had been spending the summer in one of the re-thatched old Whipsnade elephant houses while the work was being carried out. Now suddenly, they were joined by three others and the Senior Elephant Keeper, evacuated to Whipsnade for safety.

The first shock, on that fateful day, was the closing of the Park. Apart from eight Christmas Days it hadn't closed any other day since its opening. Now the Park Policeman was sent, pedalling round on his bicycle, to find the thirty-nine visitors who had preferred coming to Whipsnade rather than listen to the Prime Minister's broadcast, to tell them the Park was closing at midday. It stayed closed for the whole week.

London sent other animals down to Whipsnade, including four chimps, who were put in a makeshift pen in a garage by the office, two Orang-Utans and two Giant Pandas to join the one which had come earlier in the year. Four pandas had been sent to the Park in May. Three were Red Pandas, small reddish brown animals, with thick tails and pretty white faces, about the size of large cats, and their 'cousin' which had thick white fur with black markings and was about the size of a small bear.

There had been great excitement pre-War, nationwide, when 'Ming' the first Giant Panda ever to be seen alive in Europe had come from China to the London Zoo. Furry toy 'Mings' had been sold in the Zoo shop, rivalling the Teddy Bear for popularity. Now, as evacuees, Ming and another panda joined our Whipsnade residents. Put in a pen by the Elephant House, they plodded about, gazing through the mesh with soulful expressions on their faces, emphasised by the large black patches round their eyes. Or, with an air of deceptive docility, would sit placidly munching bamboo branches especially grown for them in Cornwall.

Giant Panda.   /BP

But the Zoological Society didn't only evacuate animals; it sent the wives and children of its London staff to be housed in the bachelor quarters at the Bothy and in the Army huts normally occupied by the summer waitresses, now no longer needed. These London Zoo wives must have found communal living difficult enough, but they also had to face the same rural problems that had confronted my mother and Mrs Macdonald when they had moved to Whipsnade, for nothing much had changed in the meantime.

For the children, however, it must have seemed like an extended summer holiday. Instead of the pavements of Camden Town and Islington, they now had the grass of the village green and common to play on and although some of them were familiar with zoo animals, many came into contact with sheep and cows for the first time in their lives. They explored the fields, picking wild flowers. Scrambled up high banks of lanes whose hedgerows were laden with rose-hips,

'The Masque of Empire', a patriotic play produced by Mrs Beal and performed by the village children and the evacuees in the Restaurant Cloisters.
Back row left to right: Mary Billet, *, Gertrud Strick, Brenda Blount, Renee Shelley, Laura Beal, *, Lily Strick.
Middle row: Jane Brettell, *, Lionel Turvey, *, Derek Alderson, Billy Beal as
St. George, I am Britannia, Herbert Strick St. Patrick, John Billett, *, *,
Front row: Gladys Cavanagh, Ann Aldridge, Rosemary Blount, Christine Coles, Francis Chute, Beryl Rogers, John Macdonald, Gillian Alderson, Florence Cavanagh.

Mary and John Billett were the children of the Keeper of the Bird Sanctuary. Ann Aldridge and Renee Shelley daughters of London Zoo keepers. Frank, Renee's father, later transferred to become an Overseer at Whipsnade. Laura and Billy were the Superintendent's children, Beryl Rogers daughter of Bert the giraffe keeper, John Macdonald son of the Park's first Overseer. Francis Chute lived at 'Sallow Spring', the Blount girls and Christine Coles in Dunstable, Jane Brettell, whose father was 2 I/C to Captain Beal in the Home Guard, lived in Dagnall. The three Stricks were Austrian refugees, from Vienna. The rest of the cast apart from Lionel Turvey were evacuees, and I'm sorry I can't remember all their names as it was a very long time ago.

clusters of crimson haws interwoven with the fluffy wild clematis 'old man's beard'. They gathered ripe blackberries and did battle with shiny conkers threaded on lengths of string. A whole new wonderland of extended freedom surrounded them, until someone thought to re-open the village school! For many years Whipsnade Village School had been closed and was by now a private dwelling house. Children from the village were either bussed to Ashton School in Church Street, Dunstable, or their parents made other arrangements for them. Now, with too many children to bus to Ashton, itself overstretched with evacuees, the Village Hall was turned into a school under the supervision of an evacuee Headmistress from London.

More children in the village meant parties and concerts and there were now enough girls for Mrs Beal to form a Girl Guide Company and a Brownie Pack. The 1st Whipsnade Guide Company, with its Headquarters in the Zoo itself, had a very adventurous War. Mrs Beal, an ex-Army wife who'd lived many years in West Africa, encouraged our outdoor activities and even sent us out on Home Guard manoeuvres as signallers and messengers. Sometimes, we were on all night exercises, which meant a few hours sleep, snatched on the

The 1st Whipsnade Guide Company photographed after winning the Dunstable District Guide Competition.
Back row left to right: Elizabeth Schuermeir, Patsy Cavanagh, me, Beryl Rogers, Pat Sines, Jane Bretttell, Esther Schuermeir.
Front Row: Florence and Gladys Cavanagh, Elsie Rogers, Mrs Beal, Mary Billet, Joan Gill, Gillian Alderson

wooden office floor close to the telephone switchboard, waiting for instructions, and finishing up with a breakfast of poached eggs and haddock, prepared by the Zoo Chef.

The Estate Office was the Headquarters of both the Home Guard and the local Air Raid Defence, with Captain Beal in command of both. It was also an Air Raid Warning Post. Warnings were phoned through to be passed on to Kensworth, Studham and the Works' Yard where the five o'clock hooter, high on the side of the water tower, served as the Air Raid siren. The wind carried its sound for some distance and the howling of the wolves, which always accompanied it, day or night, must have added both to its effectiveness and its eeriness.

Back in khaki. 'Major' Beal, OC 'D' Company, Home Guard. /LB

The Park itself suffered little damage. Some forty-one bombs were dropped on three separate occasions between August and October 1940, most of them falling in the undeveloped areas. Some fell in paddocks, making large holes in the earth, some of which were later utilized as ponds. One landed in the middle of Duke's Avenue, tearing a crater across the road and damaging a water main. The only reported casualties from all three raids were a spurwinged goose – the oldest inhabitant – and a baby giraffe which so panicked that it ran itself to exhaustion and developed pneumonia. Four months later, Rosie gave birth prematurely, losing the calf, but, it was not thought that this was as a result of the air raids.

At the same time as these raids, Harry Rance had a near miss whilst in the Axis deer paddock, Flint Pit. He reported machine gun bullets whizzing past him, causing the deer to stampede. Incidentally, when the German/Italian alliance became known as the 'Axis', the little deer, from India, were considered to have a very unpatriotic name and were referred to as the 'Spotted deer' for the duration.

The only other wartime damage to the Park was inflicted by our own troops. The army used the area in the vicinity of Bison Hill as a practice ground for tanks. Frequently, I would lie in bed, listening to the huge vehicles grinding their way along in the dark. One night I was startled by a crash, followed by silence, then a great commotion. Slipping out of bed and peering through a crack in the blackout, I could just make out the shape of a tank embedded in our garden fence. There was a great deal of shouting and engine revving, until eventually it was disentangled from the wire and the tank went on its way leaving a much buckled boundary fence in its wake. Some days later a fatigue party came to help with the repairs. They weren't the first soldiers at the Zoo. Some Royal Engineers had come after the bombing to detonate unexploded bombs.

Earlier on, it had been realised that the lion, being a well-known landmark, could be used by enemy planes to navigate their way to London or the factories of Luton and Dunstable, all working flat out on war weapons, and troops were sent to camouflage it with nets, manure and brushwood in an attempt to make it look like a chalk pit. Spicers Field, with its acreage larger than the London Zoo, would have made a good landing ground for enemy troop carrying gliders, so posts were driven into the ground at intervals as a preventative measure. One Saturday, an American fighter plane crashed in the gardens of Phil Bates and Albert Cole at the Chequers Cottages in the Bothy Block. The plane came down on the cabbages and flower beds beside a tree less than twenty yards from the two houses. There was little damage to the houses but the young pilot was killed.

The most serious damage however, during the War years, was caused by a gale in January 1943, which swept through the Park, bringing hail and sleet in its wake. In the twenty-four hours, or so, that it raged it tore down half a dozen large conifers, lopped the tops off nine more and rent a massive hole in the Cloisters' roof. When it came to be repaired it was discovered that it hadn't been looked at since being converted. The laths were rotten and the tile nails eaten through with rust. After the repairs were finished it was estimated that the roof should last another fifty years. Unfortunately, in the repairing, the beautiful mauve wisteria, which had trailed from the Cloisters' roof was destroyed.

The Cloisters became the winter Headquarters of the Whipsnade Miniature Rifle Club, which had been created from the necessity for the Home Guard to have shooting practice, once they were armed. Captain Beal was in command of the Home Guard, but there was no way he could persuade my father to join the 'toy soldiers', as he called them, and drill with broom handles; as, in fact, they had to do in the early days whilst they were still called the Local Defence Volunteers.

My father, however, became his right-hand man in the ARP and the relationship between the Air Raid Warden and the Home Guard Platoon, depicted in the television series 'Dad's Army' is, in my memory, very aptly portrayed.

Once the Home Guard had rifles however, they needed an area for target practice. The Cloisters, well protected by sandbags, was an excellent venue. It seemed a pity not to use it to the full, so the ARP and interested civilians formed themselves into the Rifle Club. The club fared well in contests against both the Home Guard and the RAF Regiment, who sometimes camped on the common, and frequently beat them. In the summer, when the Cloisters was needed for serving refreshments, the rifle range was transferred to a large chalk pit on the side of the Downs near the Bison Paddock.

This pit had previously been the site of a funeral pyre. Disaster had struck as the first Christmas of the War approached. The polar bear gave birth to a cub which was eaten by its father. Then the Black rhinoceros, which had been brought to Whipsnade amid much excitement in the spring and was one of the most valuable animals in the Park, died. The first task after Christmas was to dispose of the body. No easy task, since this species can weigh as much as three and a half tonnes. The only way was to burn it and the most suitable place was the chalk pit close to Bison Hill. A foraging party gathered wood and the body was prepared. On the first day of the burning an African elephant died and its body had to be added to the pyre. The first New Year of the War was greeted with the acrid smell of burning flesh and the belching forth of black smoke, which lasted for almost a week, until a pile of smouldering ash was all that remained of the great beasts.

There were no visitors during this time as, having closed for the first week of the war, it was shut again for the first winter from October 31st until mid February. During these months, when the Park was isolated, Billy, Laura and I had riding lessons on the Shetland ponies. I was lucky enough to graduate to Julian Huxley's Iceland ponies.

That winter was very severe. A litter of tiger cubs and one of the Giant pandas developed fits and Boxer, the two year-old giraffe, fell sick. Things looked very bleak as the cold increased and snow, once more, engulfed the Park. Ice was thick on the ponds, drinking holes had to be hacked out each day. Whipsnade looked like a winter fairyland to me under its white blanket, with the tree branches weighed down with snow and dead bracken fronds encased in crystal. To my delight, the roads were blocked, which meant that I couldn't get to school. However, what was fun for me was a hard time for the keepers, dragging straw and food across the snow to the animal pens and sheds. In addition, there was the increased worry as to how the animals would be fed if the war went on for long. The earlier hope that 'It will be all over by Christmas' had not materialised.

The Zoological Society's bank balance in 1939 had been healthy enough, but the outbreak of war had meant fewer visitors ... Things picked up, after a while, but grew worse again with the air raids of 1940. By the time the raids eased off, petrol was rationed and travel to Whipsnade became difficult. On one February day, the total gate money taken amounted to sixpence (two and a half pence), which meant that the one solitary visitor was a member of the armed forces, because they were admitted at half price. Later in the war more people found their way to Whipsnade in the summer months, glad, no doubt, to get away from it all in the peaceful surroundings of the Park.

As animal food became scarcer, so it became more expensive. In the hope of gaining help from the public towards these rising costs, the Society launched an adoption scheme. People were invited to adopt an animal of their choice and to pay for its food. Adopters were acknowledged by having their names displayed on the animal's paddock or house. The scheme got off to a good start, but support dwindled after about three years. In his 1939 Guide Book, Julian Huxley had said that visitors might give herbivores lettuce, cabbage and carrots and the bears buns and the elephants sugar and buns ... But, who could spare any of these in times of rationing?!!

The Government having brought in a wartime regulation that a certain amount of grassland must be used for growing food, the Society decided to cultivate the undeveloped area of the Park. Hay had always been made, from the beginning; now the old farmland was put back to its original use as a hundred and sixty acres came under the plough, unfortunately including the cricket pitch! The men had formed a Sports and Social Club in the early days and had been given the use of a patch of land near the common, just above the Chequers Cottages. The Care Centre now stands on what was once the Sports Field, its smart brick buildings where once an old bus, covered with wattle hurdles, served as a Pavilion.

The wartime 'Daily Occurrence Sheets' read like a farmer's diary. Potato lifting at the end of September and into October. The root crops were good ... vegetables were supplied to the Restaurant as well as being used for animal food. March and April saw hedges and bushes cut and burned. In May, there was the first scything of grass and the castrating of lambs. The breeding of domestic animals was all part of the farming programme. Pigs and sheep were sold to the Ministry of Food and the Herts. and Beds. Bacon Factory at Hitchin. Chartley and Chillingham calves were supplied to the Catering Department along with deer. Coloured calves, among the white cattle and white fawns, born to Red Deer, all had to be culled, or they would have, ultimately, spoiled the future herds. My stepmother, Edna, worked in the Estate Office during the war and tells me they all became heartily sick of venison constantly being served in the Staff Canteen. Later, they were fed a surfeit of goat! The occasional bison and even on one occasion bear made a welcome change! The more exotic Jungle fowl, seem to have been reserved for the Regent's Park Menu, as were over a hundred Chinese water deer. Turkeys and the occasional pig were sold to members of staff.

There were a couple of outbreaks of Foot and Mouth disease in the area. This was always serious, even before the Society was farming on a large scale, because this dreadfully contagious disease also affects other cloven hoofed animals as well as cattle, pigs and sheep. Very strict precautions were always taken as so many of the Park's animals were at risk. Large mats, soaked in disinfectant, were laid across all the entrance gates. No person, or vehicle, could get into the park without crossing them. Wheels were sluiced or brushed over from buckets of disinfectant kept by the gates. These strict precautions worked, the Park was never infected.

June saw hay making. The sheep were sheared, then dipped in July and August. Grass was scythed again in August and the grain was harvested. There were, of course, no giant combine harvesters then. All the children had to lend a hand gathering in the crop. I can remember my back aching, my arms sore from scratches, as we gathered up the sheaves and stacked them in stooks. A stook was made up from about seven sheaves propped against each other, heads close together, stalks slightly splayed, so that any rain ran down them and the ears could dry out as they stood through the long days of British Double Summer time. A threshing machine had been installed in the carpenter's workshop in the Works Yard and once dry enough the harvest was carted there. The grain was stored in the Army huts and the straw stacked in ricks in the Car Park, to be used later for animal bedding and fodder.

Only a few of the London keepers' wives stayed at Whipsnade for very long. Those who remained were easily housed in the Bachelors'

Bothy and a couple of cottages in the village. The furniture was removed from the Army huts, the partitions shifted and they were transformed into good dry storage barns. Throughout the year, grain, mostly oats, was bagged up and taken down to Thorne's Mill, to be ground into flour.

Because my reward was a ride on the back of the lorry down to Eaton Bray, I spent many long hours filling the grain sacks. Such was the joy, standing like Boadicea, leaning on the cab as we sped down Bison Hill with the wind on my face, that I worked happily in the storage huts, with complete disregard for the fact that I could well encounter a rat or a mouse. Strangely, I never did. On the return journey, we brought back large rough loaves of oaten bread. In Health Food shops, to my amusement, I now see people paying well over the odds for the kind of bread that was fed to the animals during the war.

Everything had to be harvested. Small wonder then, that Mrs Haine, of Dell Farm, was not at all pleased when the parakeets plundered her apple crop. There was, by then, a well-established colony living in their large communal nest in Wood Lawn Bird Sanctuary. The huge nest, which I always thought of as a block of bird 'Flats', was in a tree overhanging the Main Gate. There was constant screeching as flashes of bright green darted in and out or hovered in the branches. Anyway, they found their way down the hill and stripped Mrs Haine's orchard. The next year Keeper Billet had to catch the flock of Quaker parakeets and keep them safely behind mesh fencing until her apple crop had been harvested. Maybe, the birds resented this treatment, for by the following spring, they had flown the Park. Two were found dead in August but the fate of the rest forever remained a mystery.

So successful was the Society's farming programme in providing animal food, it was decided to continue it after the war until such time as the land was needed for Park development. The Great Whipsnade Railway now runs on land where once waved field after field of golden corn. But in spite of all these efforts, some animals had to be put down, including three elephants, one of whom was Bhisca Peary, who had come with Mangal as a baby before the war. The meat shortage also hit hard and some of the Bostock lions had to be destroyed. Pre-war, old horses were slaughtered on the premises, in the Slaughter House, in the Works' Yard. Now even these were scarce. Consignments of condemned meat, marked with a green dye, to show it was unfit for human consumption, were sent in whenever they were available. There was no fruit for the gibbons, Rhesus monkeys and chimps.

Tiny Tim.   /LM

Very early on in the war three chimps on the Chimp island were sent to Toronto. Once they had gone, the London Zoo chimps were taken from their makeshift home in the garage and set free on the island. One of these, Tiny Tim, was a mischevious little character. While he was living in the garage, he would seize every opportunity to slip through the keeper's legs and out of the gate to freedom. He must, I think, have been the cheeky chimp which swam off the island, the day I was selling postcards. Albert Blake loved him, carrying him around whenever he had the chance, the little chimp's arm fondly

70

curved round his neck. Cuddling each other thus, he often took the little animal into the office to see the office girls, until one day Tim leapt out of his arms causing havoc. The Captain was not well pleased!

However, once on the island, his antics were curtailed ... or so everybody thought! One February morning, a few years later, the keepers opened the chimps' quarters for the day and were astonished to find a baby chimp nestling contentedly among them. No one had any idea that one of the females was pregnant. An incident which cause much amusement and ribald comment among their colleagues on the other sections and the Works staff. Hurriedly one of them fetched the Captain, who stood open-mouthed, momentarily speechless. Recovering himself, he swung round on Herbert Peppiat, who had reported the birth, and with colourful expletives, asked how on earth it could have happened ... the only male was Tiny Tim ... surely he wasn't capable of fatherhood?! 'Well don't look at me!' Herbert, the small snub-nosed Keeper with the bright little eyes, retorted.

As a child, I often thought how much some of the keepers resembled their animal charges. Giraffes have beautiful eyes. Although Bert Rogers had bright blue eyes, they are the one feature of him I can remember. In fact, that was how I recognised Maureen White, in the Zoo shop, to be his granddaughter. Albert Cole always walked with the dignity of a camel. Jesse Grey loped across the Downland with the rhythm of a big cat.

CHAPTER 6

Peace and the End of an Era
(late forties)

1945 started with the familiar pattern of frost and snow. Once more unable to get through to school, I was dispatched with a crow bar to break the ice on the small pond, in Round Close, now Lake Daedulus. Cadging a lift on the snow plough, I promptly fell off the back of it as it slithered down Cut Throat Hill. One of the Italian prisoners of war on the snow plough grabbed my ankles and together he and his companion pulled me back on.

We had, at that time, two Italian prisoners working at the Zoo. During hostilities there had been a very large POW camp for Italians in Bedford but, since Italy's surrender in September 1943, they were no longer treated as enemy aliens. Because of the continuing fighting they could not, however, be repatriated either. Consequently, they were now given agricultural work in the area and Whipsnade had been allocated a couple. They were dropped off each morning by lorry and collected again in the afternoon.

Whipsnade was a fairly cosmopolitan place during the war years. There was the, to me, awe-inspiring Rudolph Wacker, in black tie and tails, dark hair sleeked back, the Head Waiter since the Park had opened. Now, we discovered, he was a German national – an enemy alien! However, because he had lived in England for so long, he was not interned, although he nevertheless had to report every week to the Police Station in Dunstable. The Catering Storeman and the Head Chef were both French. The Catering Manager, who at that time was in charge of both Regent's Park and Whipsnade, was Swiss, as was his daughter Rita, who sometimes had riding lessons with us. In the village, Colonel Chute's wife Emerine, who lived at 'Sallow Spring' and ran the Brownie Pack, was American. A Swedish lady with an unpronounceable name lived at 'Frog Corner' for a while. There were several Jewish children, refugees from Germany, Austria and

Czechoslovakia, among the evacuees from London. Such were the terrific snowfalls that, I remember, one year some of them made a large snowman on the common above 'Dell Farm' where they were billetted, and it was well into June before the last traces of it finally disappeared.

In 1945, a fox again got into the Park, killing some jungle fowl and a Canada goose. Inspection revealed that the fox must have gained access where the snow had drifted and piled high against the boundary fence in Sir Peter's Way. In due course, the fox was caught.

Among 'incidents' recorded in that year, Foot and Mouth restrictions were lifted and a Père David deer's antlers measured one inch in length!!

A very special baby ... a Père David's deer fawn.   /BP

This last, may seem a very insignificant thing to have been recorded but these fawns were, indeed, very special, since they belonged to a species of which none had been seen in the wild since 220AD in China! However, in the spring of the previous year, the Duke of Bedford had sent four of these baby deer to Whipsnade to be hand-reared. At that time, they were breeding well in Woburn Park and it was the Duke's ambition to establish a herd in America. Since they were highly nervous creatures and in the 1940s the tranquilizing of animals to facilitate moving them from place to place had yet to be developed, it was decided that the safest and surest way to send the deer any great distance would be to take them from their mothers at birth, and hand rear them. The Duke negotiated with the Zoological Society and an arrangement was made for the fawns to be brought to Whipsnade. The species had been thought to be extinct until, one day in 1865, a keen naturalist, the French missionary Armand David, caught a glimpse of them. Imagine his excitement at seeing deer that no one else, outside the Emperor's Imperial Hunting Park near Peking, had seen for over sixteen hundred years, and he made special arrangements to send skin and bone specimens back to Paris to support his story! Finally, between 1869 and 1890, live specimens were actually sent from China to European zoos – and how fortunate, for the species, this was to prove. For, during extensive floods in 1895, many of the Chinese Royal herd were drowned. The few that managed to reach ground high enough to survive were slaughtered by troops who broke into the Hunting Park on their way to relieve the Foreign Legation during the Boxer Rebellion five years later. The few that escaped this slaughter were rounded up in the Ili district. The Duke of Bedford wanted some for Woburn, where a herd was steadily being established. However, of those sent to him, only one survived as far as Tua Yuan Fu. So the Père David deer, as they were now known in honour of the man who had re-discovered them, were declared extinct in the wild, but they had been saved for posterity by the unlikely combination of a French Monk and an English Peer. Small wonder, that the progress of the first set of antlers was so carefully recorded!!

Towards the end of their first year at Whipsnade, there had been another outbreak of Foot and Mouth disease. The mats soaked in disinfectant had gone down with even greater urgency. Goats were brought in to ensure a constant supply of milk for the baby deer and Phil Bates had been appointed to the role of Head Wet Nurse! Many young keepers in their apprenticeship days helped in the bottle feeding down the years. Like human babies, the animals had to be fed every four hours at first. Angus Macdonald had retired at the end of the war and Phil, as the newly appointed Overseer, moved into the cottage next door to us. 'There goes Phil for the ten o'clock feed,' we would say as we heard his assistants from the Bothy calling for him and the little group making their way along the path at the bottom of our garden, behind the beech hedge.

After the war ended there were changes in the Catering Department. Mr Schorno took his family back to Switzerland and the recently de-mobbed Squadron Leader Teddy Rhodes became the Whipsnade Catering Manager.

On July 2nd 1945, our first summer of peace was shattered by the news that Sir Peter had died. Dr Vevers later told us that he had been in the London office when someone rushed in to tell him that an elderly gentleman had been knocked down by a taxi outside. Hurrying into the street to see what help he could give, he was shocked to discover that the white-haired figure lying in the road was his dear friend Peter Chalmers Mitchell. It was a dull, rainy day at Whipsnade the day he died, almost as though the Park was shedding silent tears for the departure of its creator. Strangely enough, it was also the seventeenth anniversary of the granting of the Royal Assent for his dream to go ahead.

As a member of the 'Cremation Society', Sir Peter was cremated, in itself causing some comment. Cremation was considered fairly radical, only legal in Britain for sixty years and practised, in the main, in free-thinking circles! He had arranged that, since Corbett – my father – had done so many odd jobs for him in the past, he should perform the last one by digging a grave for his ashes. He left precise instructions as

'Little Stonehenge'. Sir Peter's tomb.

to its size and position. Until now, there had always been considerable rumours and speculation as to the purpose of 'Little Stonehenge', the plot in Sir Peter's Way, on the brow of the hill, where he had started his tour of Hall Farm with the Council in 1926. The monument, consisting of four upright, roughly hewn, stone pillars, some eight to ten feet high, with other similar stones laid on the tops of them, overlooked the path which he had originally intended should be the main Avenue into the Park. It faced a deeply wooded bank which rose up to the plateau where the Huxleys had had their hut until their departure in 1942. A wood where, in spring, the cuckoo called, wood pigeons cooed softly and at night owls hooted against the dark silhouettes of the trees. Trees, which when we shouted, eerily threw back our distorted voices. Here, beneath this monument, my father dug the tiny grave, which I, kneeling on the thyme-scented bank, lined with soft green moss.

Peace saw the return of staff who had been away at war.

The two first to go in 1939 had been Territorials, Francis (Lol) Gladman, who had joined the Zoo in 1932 as a telephone boy, and Percy Adams. Now Lol came back and joined the camel section where he anxiously waited for the chance to transfer to the elephants. His love of these creatures had been awakened whilst serving in the Beds. Yeomanry, when he became a prisoner of the Japanese working with them on the Burma railway. He was destined to stay with elephants till his retirement in 1968. Percy, the young chimpanzee keeper from Kensworth, had also been sent to the Far East and was reported missing in Malaya. Subsequently we learnt that he too became a prisoner of the Japanese and died of dysentry in a POW camp in 1943.

Ken Smith, on the other hand, was new to the Park. He arrived after de-mob from the RAF. He was soon able to ease the new Overseer's responsibilities for feeding the Père David deer and sometimes he let me help him. On one occasion he gave me an eighteen inch ice-bound baby alligator to revive! For what seemed to me like hours, I sat in one of the little sheds in the Works Yard bathing it with warm water. At length, I was dismally forced to admit defeat. Only as I wandered off, disconsolately, through the wood, did I suddenly wonder just what would have happened if it had revived!? At other times, he would send me to feed the solitary sea lion, Alec, who lived on what had been the Chimp Island. I developed a great affinity for Alec and soon learnt to copy his bark. Entering the far end of Whipsnade Wood, with my bucket of fish, I would call out to him. Immediately recognizing my voice he replied and we would keep up our barking love calls until I arrived at the water's edge, where he was waiting for me, his sleek black body quivering in anticipation for his fish.

Whipsnade, with its soft rolling grass, daffodil-drenched banks, blossom-laden trees and little woods and coppices, has ever been an idyllic paradise for lovers, human and animals alike, as the many romances over the years have proved.

Perhaps the first of these we knew about was when Bert Matthews, Bear Keeper and stalwart of the cricket team, bowled over Dr Vevers' children's nanny, Winifred. Theirs was the first marriage I remember, followed by Carnivore Keeper, Frank Meakins and waitress Grace. I shall not list all the others, sufficient to say that my schoolfriend

Win and Bert Matthews at the time of their engagement.

Margaret had no idea when Denny Cutler returned from the RAF that she would one day be his wife, or war-time office girl, Edna, that she'd meet up with my father again when he was widowed and, in marrying him, become my stepmother! When marrying Gerry Stanbridge's daughter, Andy White became a third generation keeper, for her grandfather had been Bert Rogers, Keeper of the giraffes. As I write, there are, at the very least, a dozen people on the staff who have met their partners through the Park, including Cliff Tack who married Children's Zoo Hostess, Mary Heath. Small wonder that they laughingly call it the Marriage Bureau!

Until now, keepers, for the most part, as I have previously said, had been farm labourers or stockmen who had changed their domestic charges for more exotic animals. A young lad coming to the Park would be attached to a section and, provided he stayed the course, as those senior to him died, or retired, he might eventually aspire to become head of a section himself. Now young men were flocking into all departments, including some to study catering and one, in particular, who was designated as a 'Student Keeper'. But as there didn't seem to me to be any real promotional prospects and since I couldn't see what there was to study in mucking out and putting food and water into sheds and paddocks, I thought this title to be a very grandiose one indeed. However, I hadn't met this unique 'Student Keeper' then.

Billy, Margaret and I were lounging around idly on the oatsacks in the food store, keeping out of Storekeeper Iris's way and nibbling animal biscuits whilst planning our next adventure, when a slim young man with unusual blue eyes came in to collect food for his section. His long fair hair fell over his forehead and he was wearing suede shoes. To me, he looked more like a poet than a keeper! It transpired, when we knew him better, that it was his older brother, Lawrence, who was the poet. Gerald Durrell was a naturalist. All his life, he told us, he had been obsessed with the living creatures around him and, as he'd been born in India and lived for many years on the Greek island of Corfu, I knew he would have met some really interesting creatures and people as well.

One of the people to catch my imagination was his brother's friend Theo, who had been Gerry's tutor, and what a good teacher he must have been, for Gerry, who said he'd never been to school, seemed to know a great deal more about everything than the three of us who had! Now, he had come to the Zoological Society of London's country branch – Whipsnade – to learn all about the larger animals he couldn't keep at home. The keepers were to be his tutors, or so he mistakenly believed, for his burning ambition was to be a wild animal collector. We'd heard of Wilfred Frost and Cecil Webb, the great White Hunters, but this was our first encounter with anyone aspiring to such a dangerous and thrilling occupation!

Those of you who have seen the television series, 'My Family and Other Animals' will understand what a captivated audience we were, as this new person in our midst told us about his early life. He related splendid stories as we sat, spellbound, on the oatsacks or on the grass in the more private seclusion of Sir Peter's Way. He expounded, at length, his pet theories on the care of animals in captivity, and anyone who has visited his Zoo in Jersey will know he subsequently put many of these into practice.

Bill Beal

Gerald Durrell back from his first collecting trip. I believe the little creature on his shoulder was quite rare and was called an Awantibo.

With Margaret and two live Teddy Bears.

On August evenings, when the Park was closed, we trooped out onto the Downs to watch Gerry, the great collector to be, in action. Hidden among the bushes we watched while he practised on the wallabies. The unsuspecting creatures grazed peacefully where they had slept for most of the day, giving the illusion that the grass was dotted with grey/ brown furry hillocks. Gerry lay still, breathing slowly and evenly, the subdued shades of his clothing and almost straw-coloured hair blending into the dried grass between the Tiger Pit and the Lion's Den. Snakelike, he slid smoothly and swiftly towards his prey, suddenly seizing it by the tail. Then there followed a violent tug-of-war, during

An unsuspecting wallaby. /LM

which both contestants bounced across the hill, etched against the skyline. The wallaby angrily thrashing its tail, Gerry hanging on, bobbing about on the end of it, on his haunches, or being dragged full length across the grass, but never releasing his determined grip. Until at last wearied by the conflict, knowing it would never get the better of this man, the wallaby gave in.

The slim, aesthetic young man was a great deal tougher than he looked. None of us had any doubt he would ultimately achieve anything he set his sights on. However there were times when he wondered if he would actually live to see the day. Gerry often felt that some of the keepers took careless risks with his life. 'Familiarity breeds contempt', not that keepers feel contempt for the animals! It is simply that constant, day-to-day contact can make them so familiar

Hoping to escape.   /BP

with their charges that they tend to forget how dangerous some of them can be.

Cat lover that I am, my hair stands on end when I recall Graham Lucas's description of climbing up a ladder to rescue a cheetah from a tree – they are good at climbing up, but hopeless at getting down again – then finding himself safely, after a minor balancing feat, on *terra firma* but alone and undefended in its cage with the big startled cat! Although he swears the cat was more scared of him! Incidents such as this worried Gerry although, no doubt, now, after so many years of handling dangerous animals himself, he has a better understanding of those men of his early days in Zoology.

Not that some were anxious to teach him much. He couldn't have known how, in the early days, the countrymen had eyed the newcomers from the London Zoo with deep suspicion, for this attitude had mellowed over the years. Now, not only were their own village boys returning from the war with their horizons widened, but there was an entirely new breed of educated man slipping into their ranks. Small wonder that they wanted to keep what knowledge they had to themselves. They were afraid for their jobs. He hadn't bargained for this canny closeness towards him. He'd expected them to be like his tutor Theo, anxious to impart all the knowledge they had.

By the way he used to speak, I think Gerry was disappointed too at the lack of scientific expertise about the place at that time. It was obvious from the outset that he and Ken Smith would develop a rapport. In later years, Ken joined Gerry for a while in Jersey and they have been on at least one collecting trip together. Gerry Durrell's book

Visiting Ken Smith with my first two children, Rebecca and Paul, many years later
when Ken was the Director of Paignton Zoo, Devon (circa 1959). /GS

'The Bafut Beagles' was dedicated to Ken.

Gerry's stay at Whipsnade was brief, but he had brought a new dimension to our lives. Margaret and I have one hilarious memory of him. VJ Night was celebrated with a huge bonfire on the common. In the darkness of the summer evening the four of us evolved a lively, boisterous game, until she and I, in a desperate attempt to prevent ourselves being beaten, tripped Bill and Gerry, pitching Gerry head-first into a large, soft, ripe, cow patch. The cleaning up operation took place in the long-suffering Mrs Beal's kitchen and the smell was far more pungent that any of her husband's curries! We often wonder whether this early fertilisation contributed, in some small way, to his ultimate success and world-wide fame !?

Meanwhile, major construction work was getting underway. At the Fellows' Pavilion, which had been boarded up for use by the Home Guard as a look-out post because of the splendid view it afforded across the valley, the shutters came down. The Bar and Still were removed and replaced by perches. In no time, it was once more full of life, as rows of brightly coloured macaws screeched their welcome and white cockatoos sagely nodded their golden crests where Fellows had previously nodded their heads over whisky and afternoon tea.

The Tiger Pit was converted to receive two very different new occupants, Kam and Chatka, Kodiak bears. There was great excitement as the large wooden crates holding these two enormous bears (they can weight up to one thousand, seven hundred and twenty pounds each) were lowered by crane into the deep pit. These shaggy bears, native of Kodiak Island in the Gulf of Alaska, are the biggest of all bears. They are also the largest meat-eating animals in the world that live on land. It was a pity really, that they had to go into the pit. For at a depth of twenty feet their sheer size of over nine feet in height could never be fully appreciated.

They were housed next door to other creatures from the frozen North, the polar bears, who lived on simulated ice floes, constructed from reinforced concrete. All traces of this Pen and the Tiger Pit have now disappeared, as both have be infilled and grassed over. There was always a vast number of onlookers thrilled by the aquatic antics of these great white bears. They so obviously had so much fun, plunging in and out of their pool and playing with their rubber tyres and sticks, that their pleasure naturally spilled over to the onlookers, as did the spray of fishy water when, with their 'act' over, one of them would come across to the bars, vigorously shaking the moisture everywhere as it acknowledged the audience's applause, nodding its beautiful head, delight shining in its eyes. Along with these crowds, I have spent many a happy hour watching their performance and their obvious happiness, because they were active and responding gleefully to public adulation.

The polar bears having fun with an old tyre. All traces of the pool (where my father once bathed) and the concrete pen have now disappeared. Whipsnade's last Polar bears were sent to Chester in 1984. /LB

Some of the visitors worried because the male spent a lot of his time walking backwards and forwards, shaking his head from side to side. They thought he was bored. The keepers told them that, in the wild, the male behaves in precisely this same way, patrolling backwards and forwards in front of the cave where the female was having her young, thus keeping the entrance from being blocked by snow.

Perhaps that was why, initially, Whipsnade's polar bear cubs were eaten by their father!? It is now known that the pregnant female goes off and hibernates by herself to give birth, usually to a pair of cubs, which she keeps with her for two years, teaching them to fend for themselves and keeping them as far away from their father as possible. Eventually the problem was overcome and cubs were successfully reared. Many zoos having Polar Bear cubs find an increase in the number of visitors, as the Zoological Society was to discover with the birth of Brumas in Regent's Park in 1949. It is sad that there are no longer either Polar or Kodiak bears at Whipsnade.

The following year again brought heavy snows. Once more, Whipsnade was blocked off and a double-decker bus and Captain Beal's car were stuck in drifts on the top of Dunstable Downs for over a week! Some vehicles were always trapped in the drifts and Mrs Beal always, somehow, managed to be among them. However, in the heavy snows of 1947, Captain Beal was to announce to the office that his wife had got his b***** car stuck on the downs again!!, for the last time. He retired in April of that year. Having been the Veterinary Officer as well as Superintendent since the Park's opening, it is fitting to record that he left only two sick animals when he departed, a poorly baby bear and an elephant with an abcess!

Captain Beal, Bill and Phil Bates in the old Morris which Phil drove round the Park all day long with the roof down in all weathers – it probably wouldn't go up – whistling all the time.

CHAPTER 7

A Birthday Party and a Tragedy (the fifties)

By the time Whipsnade celebrated its 21st Birthday, the tall, dour, E H Tong had firmly held the reins for just five years. The dark, lean man was the complete opposite of plump, jovial Captain Beal, not only in looks, but also in his approach to his managerial duties. He took up residence with his wife Dorothy and small son Julian in Sir Peter's 'Russian Bungalow' at Holly Frindle.

One of my most memorable encounters with this new Superintendent, or Director, as he was later called, was when he, discovering my love for Alec the sealion and my passion for swimming, dared me to take a dip in the moat round Sea Lion Island.

The Chimp Island was by now home to the sea lions.   */BP*

I was not, however, the first person in my family to plunge into an animal pool. Some years earlier, there had been a problem in emptying the Polar Bear Pond. Coming home for his swimming trunks, my father went back to the enclosure and, satisfying himself that the bears were properly secured in their catch-up, dived in and sorted out the problem. He had come home for a bath, reeking of stale fish and polar bear oil!

I'd inherited his love of swimming and I was always ready for a dare ... This had resulted in my plunging myself into the icy waters of the Water Tower and the Reservoir. The water in the tower was so shallow I had grazed my knees on the bottom and it was intensely cold, for freshly pumped water was gushing into one corner the whole time. The reservoir was equally cold but far more terrifying. The chill waters were very deep and there was the added eeriness of swimming underground completely in the dark, save for one narrow shaft of light that spilled through the small opening.

Alec's pond was just as cold, for much as I loved him, I had no intention of going home smelling as foully as my father had done after his dip in the Polar Bear Pool, so I chose a day when the moat had been cleaned out and was being refilled with clear fresh water. Sometimes now I look at the tempting clear waters of the Dolphinarium ... If only that had been there then! ... Who knows? Perhaps one day Jim'll Fix it for me?

Since E H T was living in the bungalow at Holly Frindle, the upstairs floor of the Beals' old house was converted into a flat for the Chief Accountant and the whole of the ground floor was given over to offices, the Catering Department moving theirs across from the Restaurant complex.

One of my last 'holiday' jobs at the Zoo was checking the waitresses' bills in the Beals' old sitting room where we'd held our wartime Guide meetings. The Catering Department had undergone some radical changes. The Cloisters, where light luncheons and afternoon teas had been served in the past, now became a Cafeteria. The green tables and chairs at all the Kiosks were painted pillar box red and in the Restaurant itself the small dining room was re-decorated and, as previously mentioned, the Skeaping paintings were lost for ever.

There were still, at this time, stringent building restrictions which limited the construction of new animal houses and shelters but, nevertheless, reorganisation work continued. Wire netting fences were gradually replaced by low barriers in sunken ditches, as Sir Peter had envisaged from the beginning. Much of the undergrowth in the woods, which offered hiding places and shelter for pheasants and small roaming animals like the muntjac, was removed, thus opening up more panoramic views.

A penguin area was created on the Downs. It was quite unlike the 'Space Age' Tecton Pond in Regent's Park, but was and, in fact, still is far more natural with its rocks and scrub elder and hawthorn which shelter it from the west wind. One day, I watched with fascination the ritual of a little Humboldt penguin collecting grass for its nest among those rocks. Out it popped from a crevice between them, plunged into the pool, swam across, scrambled onto the bank, toddled to the fence and tugged at some long entwined grass with its beak. Pulling out the tough grass, it scurried back to the rocks, on dry land, around the edge of the pool – grass held triumphantly aloft in its beak. It disappeared into the crevice, then re-emerged and doggedly repeated the whole exercise – presumably all day, I didn't stop to watch – but never once while I was there did it attempt to swim with the dry grass in its beak!

The Pygmy hippos had been regular summer visitors to the pond in Spicers Field; now it was decided to see if their large cousins, the huge water-loving creatures from the steamy African swamps and rivers, could adapt to the Whipsnade climate and survive in the open Chiltern air. Holly Frindle ponds were selected for this experiment since, lying as they do in the hollow by the entrance to Sir Peter's Way at the southern end of the Park, they are sheltered from the east and west winds by the rising ground of Dagnall and Holly Frindle Paddocks. Two of these ponds, which had been home to the graceful Whooper swans, were extended and concreted to accommodate the ungainly, rounded figures of two year-old hippos Belinda and Henry who arrived at Whipsnade in 1950 and were soon immersed in the dank waters. They settled well and forty years on still blissfully occupy their own little Eden, where they have produced eighteen calves. Strangely, only one of these has been a female, although, Wendy, in her turn, bore her father another daughter, Winnie, who was eventually returned to Africa.

Surely this success proved beyond doubt Sir Peter's point that, provided they are protected from cold winds and are well fed, animals can readily adapt to alien climates. Surprisingly, these large animals, with enormous mouths and large yellow teeth, are quite placid creatures. Henry is known as the 'gentle giant' and his keepers have even seen him, from time to time, with a duckling on his nose. Males do get angry when others try to appropriate their feeding grounds. In

Henry and Belinda. /BP

the wild they feed at night, never wandering far from the water where they spend the daylight hours. The males mark the paths they traverse by flicking dung about with their tails. At sunrise, having fed on grass, which they wrench up with the strong grip of their toughened lips and a swish of their large heads, they smell their way along their trail back to the water, trotting on their surprisingly little legs.

Another huge creature, an Indian rhinoceros, arrived, and Mohan and Mohini were installed in a paddock hard by the Giraffe House. Indian rhinos seem to me to be animals that have been put into suits of

An Indian rhinoceros. /BP

armour, the folds of the thick hide giving the appearance of having been riveted together in sections and not being all of a piece! It was unbelievable, to see these massive, fierce-looking creatures settle down on the grass for Bert Rogers to attend to their hooves. Yet Indian rhinos, like hippos, are peaceful timid animals, living comparatively solitary lives and normally only charging in anger when they feel their calves are threatened. On wet days, those large hooves, carrying such a weight of body, churned up the mud at the side of their pen into small craters as they plodded up and down, staring at the fragile, two-legged, noisy specimens on the far side of their thick iron bars. At other times, they ambled down the gradual slope at the far end of their paddock, lowering themselves into their pond. Rhinos enjoy wallowing in water and mud. Their huge bodies displaced water to make a lovely slushy area for them to roll in and paddle through on their way out.

Looking across towards Central Avenue from the Rhino Paddock, one could see where a tree had been enclosed to make a home for the Red pandas. Behind the Riding Kiosk another tree had become the central point of a much larger enclosure for a colony of Rhesus monkeys. These cheeky little monkeys, with their large ears, bare faces and close deep-set eyes, performed endless antics to the delight of the hordes of onlookers gathered round their outsize cage. They ran agilely up the tree trunk, mothers with their babies clinging to their fur. They climbed the fence and chattered at the visitors, bounced up and down on their see-saw and girated gleefully on their large iron wheel.

It was a happy lively corner of the Park ... The air was constantly filled with monkeys gibbering, humans laughing, children squealing excitedly as they clung to the thick fur of the camel or pretended to be cowboys on the little, trotting, black Shetland ponies or climbed the steps and sat on the swaying houdah on the elephant's back. The elephant herd had now been increased to five.

Dixie, the old professional and possibly the oldest inhabitant, and Mangal Peary were joined by a baby, Valli, who soon sussed out that Keeper Lol Gladman kept biscuits in his pocket, and Sita Devi, a small Singalese elephant and her baby, Malini. Dixie and Mangal Peary were busy all through the long summer afternoons giving rides, while the three smaller elephants were petted and patted by the visitors on the lawn nearby.

The 21st Birthday celebrations took place all summer long, although one special week – May 19th to 25th – was set aside, during which the Park stayed open until ten o'clock each evening. Surprisingly, to me, only six hundred and fifty seven visitors were

An elephant flies in. Baby Valli being fed by her air hostess. George Braham, who came to Whipsnade with Dixie, is on the left, the keeper in the centre is Lol Gladman, whose love affair with elephants began when he was a prisoner of war in Burma. /DG

actually admitted after 6 o'clock. Although, no doubt, many stayed later than usual, many must have missed the very special magic of the Park after dusk. I personally wish it was open until ten o'clock more often!

There was a Garden Party for the Fellows in June, at which the VIPs – who had paid ten shillings and sixpence for their 'By Invitation Only' tickets – were received by Viscount Alanbrooke, the President of the Zoological Society. Their special entertainments included rides round the Park in the road train, a parade of tame animals, including ponies and camels, and a Chimpanzees' Tea Party provided by the London Zoo's 'Tea Party Chimps'. The guests partook of their own teas to the strains of the Central Band of the RAF Orchestra.

The White Lion, on a white key with a maroon background, was the 21st Birthday official logo. It was after all the symbol of the Park, standing as it still does, dominating the hillside, a sign to aircraft of an animal compound and Whipsnade's proud announcement of itself to all in the valley below. Now it was illuminated with over 1,000 coloured bulbs installed round its perimeter and the electricity supply extended down to it with the help of the Eastern Electricity Board. By

Actress Ann Todd hands Valli the 'Key of the Door' at the 'Film Stars' Tea Party', which formed part of the birthday celebrations. I thought the honour should have gone to Dixie; after all she had been a film star in her day, but apparently she was too big to get into the enclosure reserved for this function. /BT

then I was living in Totternhoe, where I was able to look out of my window each evening and see it twinkling above me like a diamond on the Downs. Nearly forty years on, for payment of £3.50 one can have it lit up by request to celebrate a special occasion.

The volume of traffic at the Bank Holiday was as overwhelming as at the first Bank Holiday in 1931. There were so many cars crawling at

The chimpanzees' tea party.   /LM

snail's pace up the hill to the Main Gate, that I decided to walk into the village. Standing on the brow of the hill above Anne's Café (now called Old Hunter's Lodge) I stared in amazement at the scene. At that time there was an RAC Box on a small island in the centre of the crossroads. That day it was isolated in a sea of gleaming metal. Cars which had been bonnet to bumper beside me from the gates and into the village, now continued in an unending stream as far as the eye could see along the New Road. The road across Whipsnade Heath was still known as the 'New Road', although it had been cut as long ago as 1931 to enable traffic to reach Whipsnade from the A5 (Watling Street) through the straight main street of Kensworth rather than the twisting narrow lane that ran from Markyate. Traffic was even attempting to crawl out of there to join another unending stream emerging from Holywell Road from Studham. To the left, Honey Furlong, which slopes gently from the Downs to the crossroads (so named from the profusion of honeysuckle which once wound itself up into the branches of the overhanging trees) was solidly blocked. The Police reported that it was possible to walk from the Main Gate to the traffic lights in the centre of Dunstable on top of the cars, and I fully believed it.

That year there were over half a million visitors, exceeding the previous highest year by some twenty thousand.

❖ ❖ ❖ ❖ ❖

The White Lion was again lit up for the Coronation, the following year. The Omugabee of the British Protectorate of Ankole in Uganda was in England for the Coronation and visited the Park where the first twin calves had been born in the herd of Ankole cattle. The Omugabee was entertained to lunch and presented with the first born bull of the herd, which he immediately deposited with the Society. In their native land, these beautiful cattle were kept, not so much for milk and beef as for their enormous horns, possibly larger than those of any other species of cattle, which taper gracefully in a slightly inward curve. Not surprisingly the horns were used extensively in bartering, especially for wives!! In 1967, the traditional rulership of Ankole ended and it became a Federal State. Besides its historical Bantu Kingdoms, Uganda had had two well-run National Parks and a Gorilla Sanctuary, all of which suffered at the hands of poachers and squatters during the 1970s and 80s. The operations of Zoos and Safari Parks all over the world, at least to some extent, prevent the extinction of some species, which might otherwise disappear, as a result of civil strife, etc. in their natural habitat.

Ankole cattle. In their native land their beautiful horns are used in bartering for brides.
/BP

The year after the Omugabee's visit, the new Duke of Bedford visited Whipsnade. He had been recalled from Africa following his father's sudden death in a shooting accident. Not only did he face crippling death duties, due to the demise of both his father and grandfather coming so unexpectedly close together, but Woburn Abbey was badly in need of restoration ... he needed money. Not long after his visit, we heard that he had opened the Abbey to visitors. Ripples of shock ran through the nation at the Russell family's action. Peers of the Realm did not open their homes to the general public!! Even more shocking was the news that a Merry-go-Round had been installed in the grounds! Soon the staff at Whipsnade dubbed him the 'Showman Duke', despite the fact that their own genteel, Park buses had been replaced by a gaudy little road train, complete with canvas top and ornate knobs. Much more in keeping with a Fairground than a learned scientific society!! Where the old Eleventh Duke had taken positive action to save species of the wild animal kingdom from extinction, the new Ducal entrepreneur took dynamic action to save his inheritance. By so doing, the grandson of one of Whipsnade Park's earliest and most generous benefactors was destined to become its nearest and most deadly rival. But in the fifties his Safari Park was an undreamed-of threat to come. In the year he opened his home to the public, Whipsnade opened its new Children's Zoo, which by the end of the fifties had proved so popular that one in four visitors went into it; its road train gave over one hundred thousand and its elephants seventy-four thousand rides.

The gaudy little road train with the canvas top and ornate knobs.   /GS

The Society sent two pairs of Père David deer to the Zoological Society of China. It will be recalled that, with the Duke's grandfather, Whipsnade had played a large part in the breeding of this near vanished species. Now they were, once more, back in their homeland. Phil Bates was awarded the Zoological Society of London's Bronze Medal for the tremendous part he had played in this achievement.

One of the delights of a visit to Whipsnade for the children was the handling of small creatures in the Children's Zoo. The little girl on the right, engrossed in the snake, is Phil Bates' niece Marilyn Hurst. To the left of the picture my daughter Rebecca is kneeling beside her friend Sara Norris. /DG

Hostess Maureen Meadows gives my son Paul a pony ride. Note the old style hostess' uniform. /DG

It was another breed of deer which, in later years, generated the greatest excitement with my young children. The wapiti, a smaller version of the moose, whom it closely resembles with its large flattened horns, also comes from North America, where it is known as the elk. The wapiti graze the mountain pastures in summer, going down into the forest valleys in winter. There had been both moose and wapiti in the Park during the fifties, but the wapiti stayed longer in their paddock on the side of the Downs. About the size of the European Red deer, people often mistakenly think that reindeer are the same size as well. This probably explains why my father, in the absence of reindeer in those days, told the children that the bull wapiti helped to pull Santa's sleigh!!! They would toddle off eagerly to the wood by Ivinghoe Gap and, pressing their faces against the fence, whisper messages for the big deer to relay to Father Christmas!!

Coincidentally, now in 1990 there is a reindeer in that same paddock, and the wapiti have gone. Most folk are surprised, coming face-to-face with Reindeer for the first time, to see how small they are. Graham Lucas, the current Lecturer on Animal Activities, explains that they have to be small – we couldn't do with eight of them on the roof, all at once, if they were any bigger! Although – as he points out – they do have large hooves, which are very useful for digging up food buried under snow and their big spreading feet support their weight on marshland, snow and, of course, on our slippery roof tiles!

The wapiti. My father told my children the wapiti helped to pull Santa's sleigh and they gave him messages to pass on to Santa. /BP

Farther along the Downs from the wapiti paddock were some new tigers from Johore. Having been released on arrival, they raced round and round their enclosure and then, according to their keepers, went to earth for several days ... This, in itself, seems unusual, for cats, large or small, usually mark out new territory. However, the Johore tigers were finally spotted stalking at dusk ... which bears out my earlier comment ... there is something extra magical about Whipsnade Wild Animal Park in the evening.

Wild as these tigers may have been, however, Frank Meakins – Head of the Carnivore Section – certainly preferred them to the little newcomer from Nuremberg, a four month old polar bear which had been exchanged for two bison. Before the day was out, he must have been one of those who dearly wished the Society had kept their bison. The *Daily Express* newspaper had adopted the cub and had run a competition to name it and from the many entries, SPITFIRE was chosen ... But neither the winner of the twenty-five pound prize nor the newspaper could have realised just how apt this name was to prove ... Spitfire duly arrived on a gentle April day and was put into her very own, especially prepared pit ... within ten minutes the inside of the pit was wrecked and the little firebrand was on her way out – proving in no uncertain terms, that no six foot pit was going to hold a ball of white, furry frenzy ... Phil Bates seized her ... struggling furiously, she sank her teeth into him as he finally thrust her back into the pit ... Out she came again ... this time, Phil let Frank have a go ... He was bitten in the leg ... She was not put back in the pit! She was eventually – still struggling furiously – shut in a nearby stall. Frank was heard to remark that he usually looked after the tigers and he wished he was with them now, as he ruefully nursed his injured leg.

No doubt the tiger he had in mind was Kaseh, the Malayan 'gift', a gentle creature which had been brought from the jungle where her mother had been shot. Frank had hand-reared her and although she was three years old she still liked him to stroke her head whilst she was feeding – small wonder he preferred her to the tiny bear so aptly named!! However, neither his nor Phil's wounds bore any comparison to the terrible injuries inflicted on a child visitor a few weeks later. That day is firmly fixed in my mind for quite another reason – it was the only time I ever succeeded in cycling non-stop from the bottom of Lancot Hill to the Zoo Main Gates without once getting off to push!!

It was the last day of May. Peals of children's laughter had rung across the Downs as a group of Cub Scouts played a game of rough and tumble ... three boys, however, were following their own pursuits … One was lying across the fine wire protective mesh, tickling a lion's ear with a stick … Not that the lion seemed to mind … most cats love having their ears tickled as Frank's Kaseh enjoyed her head being stroked … But it was two lionesses who were restive …

'It was two lionesses who were restive.'   /LM

evidently disturbed by the din two other boys were making close to the fence. They had ignored the notice forbidding them to climb over the safety barrier and were running up and down and stamping their feet … on the wrong side of it and within inches of the iron bars of the enclosure. Suddenly, provoked beyond endurance, one of the lionesses reared up. Terrified, one boy scrambled back over the barrier to safety. His companion must have panicked and lost his sense of direction, because, instead, he ran away from the lioness, but still stayed between the bars and the safety barrier … coming to a dead end he turned, but, as he retraced his steps, she thrust a huge front paw through, grabbed his ankle and with her other front paw knocked him to the ground with a single blow … A bystander vainly attempted to pull him away from her grasp, but the harder he pulled the more the lioness hung on. He had no hope of saving the boy. Then someone hit the animal with an iron bar and the child was finally dragged free. It seems he never once cried out, but simply moaned softly asking for help. He was taken to the Luton & Dunstable Hospital where both his arms had to be amputated. We listened daily to the News Bulletins for the whole week it took him to die … A shadow hung over the Park. It was the first fatal accident to a child, although the Society could in no way be held to

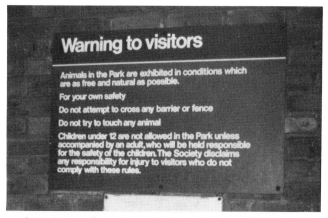

A current warning notice at the Main Entrance. (1990)   /DP

blame. Its Bye Laws have always clearly stated that children are only allowed into the Park on condition that those who bring them are responsible for their safety.

Phil Bates' great love and hobby was the breeding of Tibetan Mastiffs. Occasionally visitors would see them on a running chain by the reservoir. Bruce, black with tan markings, was my favourite. He was a great, gentle dog and he used to let me sit on his back and ride him like a small pony. But now he and Sonia, a tan bitch by whom he'd had many pups, were gone and the time had come for Phil Bates himself to leave the Park, forced into early retirement by a back injury sustained whilst having an altercation with the chimps! He moved away from his cottage next to ours the year after the wolves were moved from the pinewood at the bottom of our gardens.

My mother's 'dark forest', against the backdrop of which she had seen the first glimpse of her fairytale home, had suffered badly during the gales and storms of the ensuing thirty years. Gaps, where trees had blown down, created funnels for following gale force winds to create further havoc. The time had come to fell the remaining trees and replant the whole area. A new pack of pure Canadian Timber wolves, was installed in a new wood at the bottom of Central Avenue. The old pack established at the opening of the Park, was an in-bred mixture of Timber wolves and the larger, darker European species. The pack of tawny wolves in their lesser wood, half hidden behind Avenue Kiosk and its adjacent toilets, lack somehow the dramatic impact of the old pack in their sinister wood by the cottages.

There had been Australian dingoes in the Park for as long as I could remember; before setting off for school, I used to cycle to see them in their pen, where they came to the fence and wagged their tails in greeting. Huskies came in 1939, their solid thickly furred bodies contrasting with the lean tawny dingoes. There were about a dozen of them in a pen next to the Mongolian Wild horses on the edge of Dagnall Paddock. Some more arrived in the hail, sleet and snow of January 1942, and the following year some were loaned to the Ministry; presumably they went to war. Four were sold to an Antarctic Expedition in 1954. But, as the fifties drew to a close there was something of a purge on 'domestic' dogs.

Phil Bates was succeeded as Overseer by Owen Chamberlain, who had started working at Whipsnade on August 4th 1951. Fond of animals, always having had horses and other pets and feeling the need for a short break from the family's building business, he came to the Park 'just for a change'! Like so many 'beginners' before him, he was sent to the Bear Section, detailed to clean up the Bear Garden. Before keepers entered the bear pit, they were always careful to lock the bears away in their 'catch-up'. As Owen says, it was very necessary to have great faith in the keeper doing the locking up. His Section Leader on that first day was Bert Matthews, so he should have had no worries. However, he admits that a great deal of that day was spent looking over his shoulder in fear and trepidation!! He survived, without incident, and at the time of writing, almost forty years on, he is still enjoying his 'brief stay' at Whipsnade.

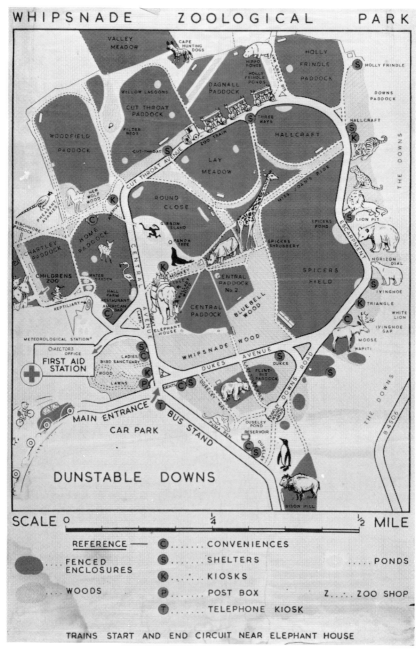

A picture map of the period. Note the wapiti in its pen on the Downs.

CHAPTER 8

The Age of the Automobile
(the sixties)

The moving of the wolves was the forerunner of the many changes which were to follow swiftly, altering forever the approach to the Park.

Whipsnade was now in the age of the automobile. Since the early days, when cars were admitted only on Mondays, people had become

With Pippa and Bill, my two younger children, at the new entrance.   */DP*

Dixie retired from riding in 1962 after having given the public yeoman service for thirty years.
                                                                                    /BP

dependant on their vehicles and were reluctant to walk anywhere they could drive. The Park had to keep up with the times. Now cars were admitted seven days a week. At first they entered through the Main Gate, but, as this was the Exit Gate as well, it limited the numbers that could pass through at any one time. Consequently, there was a considerable build-up of traffic on the approach roads. In 1960 nearly thirty thousand cars were admitted. Action was necessary. It was estimated that the yearly turnover of visitors would steadily increase to a million.

The old Clock Tower and Gate House, with its four turnstiles, invalid carriage and push-chair store, was demolished. In its place, the flat-roofed building, housing the shop, admission and Gatekeeper's office was built, together with a wide sweeping road, dividing into three car lanes with three Pay Booths. This work started in the year in which Sir Peter's Memorial Plinth was dedicated.

Dixie was once more gainfully employed moving trees to clear the ground for the new elephant paddock. /BP

The changes meant that the new entrance no longer bore any resemblance to the old Hall Farm building, but was far more in keeping with the 'futuristic' lines of the Elephant House. After the new entrance was completed, work started on an exciting new scene to welcome visitors. With the widening of the convergence of Duke's and Central Avenues, much of the edge of Whipsnade Wood had been felled and a large moated Elephant Paddock was constructed. Visitors, on entering the Park, now had an unimpeded view of Elephants spraying themselves with the reddish-brown dust, for the soil, in this area of the Park, is far less chalky than up on the Downs escarpment.

The ageing Dixie was retired from riding in 1962, when she must have been well past seventy. For a while, she stood forlornly in her concrete stable, missing the exercise from giving rides and the adulation of the crowds, which she had enjoyed throughout her working life, both here in the Park and in her Circus days. However, when the work started on the new Elephant Paddock, she again found herself gainfully employed. As the mature larch trees were felled to make the open space for the Compound, she could be seen with a smile once more on her aged features as she happily pushed and rolled the tree trunks out of the way. It is said 'Elephants never forget!' I wonder if she recalled the day, some thirty years earlier, when she rolled the Circus wagons into position, when she first arrived. By now, however, her feet were giving her trouble. No doubt, they had been wearied by the many miles she had plodded up and down the Elephant Walk over the years. I can sympathise with her, I remember how hard it was on my feet walking up and down with the Shetland ponies, and I was only a 'School Holiday' pony girl, walking on the soft grass. Her swollen feet were soaked daily in a tub of water, but the end of the line had

When I was a school holiday pony girl wearing a pair of Sir Peter's socks.

finally come for the old trouper and she died a year before the Paddock she would have enjoyed so much was completed.

The Elephant rides had stopped at Whipsnade with Dixie's retirement, although they weren't actually banned by the Zoological Society until 1966. It was felt that it was too much for Mangal Peary to carry the burden alone, and Valli had a wild streak which made her unreliable. As it was, one afternoon, a peacock flew out of nearby bushes startling Peary. Fortunately, her keeper, John Datlen, was riding on her neck and managed to bring her under control, by pressing his legs against the nerves behind her ears. He said afterwards it was an uncomfortable moment and dreaded to think what the consequences would have been had it been Valli or if the disturbance had been a low-flying jet.

Camel, pony and llama cart rides continued for a while, as Vince Curzon recalls to his chagrin. He sometimes led the llamas, Nina and Ricky, who took it in turns to pull the little cart. These two were, in the true tradition of all good llamas, very stubborn. If they felt there were too many passengers in the cart, such that they were being expected to pull too much weight, they would simply sit down on their haunches, refusing to budge until the load was lightened.

After the Elephant Paddock was brought into use, a new baby elephant, Kumara, the first to arrive since Valli in 1950, came from Bangkok. Kumara, whose name meant Princess, was only four feet tall, weighed four hundred and eighty pounds and had a sixty-four inch waist. When they are born, elephant calves are usually about two feet tall and weigh about two hundred and twenty four pounds. A two month old goat called Giselle was put with her to keep the little elephant company, not the first time a goat had been used in this way. Towards the end of the war, when the giraffe herd was reduced to one solitary animal, a fawn, shaggy goat had been put in with George! They were an odd pair to look at, but they got on very well together.

The same year that Kumara arrived, saw the tragic death of London Zoo's African elephant – Dicksie. In stretching to take food from a visitor, Dicksie had fallen into the deep moat surrounding their enclosure. This accident led to a total ban on all animal feeding by the public. Feeding of some animals had always been forbidden and there had been growing concern about the unsuitability of the food being offered. With the lifting of food restrictions the Society was becoming far more concerned about correct diets for the animals. Dicksie's death provided the opportunity it needed. Now there would be no ill feeling from the public at the ending of a practice that had lasted for

The odd couple.   /BP

generations.

Not long after, Whipsnade received two baby African elephants. Katie and Susie were only six or seven months old when they arrived in open-slatted crates, having been brought from Zambia in a British United Airways Britannia under the watchful eye of Overseer Lol Gladman. There had been such an increase in the elephant population in parts of Africa that a cull was then in progress, and Katie and Susie would have been slaughtered if the Zoological Society of London hadn't bought them from the Zambian Government's Department of Game & Fisheries. Many wild animals, elephants in particular, seem to have such 'ups and downs'. Recently there has been a great outcry against the slaughter of elephants for their ivory, to the extent that it was feared they would become extinct. Now it is reported that so many are moving towards Game Reserves, in search of food, it is feared that there will be too many for the environment to sustain them! How necessary it is to have elephants in our zoos throughout the world!

To avoid squabbles, the Park's Elephant Paddock was divided into three sections and, now that Kumara had two little friends, Giselle was sent to the Children's Zoo. Unfortunately, Susie had a liver complaint when she came and did not live for very long. The Zambian Government replaced her with two more babies, M'Tendre and M'Samua, whose Swahili names meant Peaceful One and Fierce One. These two needed hand rearing as well. In the wild, baby elephants will consume some solid food by the time they are six months old, but they still like tucking themselves between their mother's front legs suckling her milk until they are almost two years old. The keepers became substitute mothers, feeding them every four hours from six o'clock in the morning until ten at night. It wasn't practical to bring in great quantities of cow's milk to provide the couple of gallons consumed at each feed. Neither was it possible to sustain a herd of goats big enough to provide the one thousand gallons of milk they would get through before they were weaned. So the keepers resorted to powdered skimmed milk, mixed with water and carefully heated to the right temperature in their little room by the Elephant House, then put into lemonade bottles! Baby elephants do not suck through teats, they drink straight from the bottle placed in the corner of their mouths – apparently lemonade bottles have good necks which are easy for babies to grip with their tongues. Some milk was always left standing by in a bucket so that, eventually, the little animals would discover how to drink for themselves by sucking up the liquid with their trunks and squirting it into their mouths. After a while the number of feeds was reduced. Quantities of rice and eggs were gradually added to the milk and then solid food, in the form of hay and branches, was introduced.

Ask any keeper who hand rears any animal and he or she will tell you that the first feeds to go are the early morning and late evening ones! At this time, John Datlen was living in Dunstable and needed to be on his way by five-thirty in the morning to cycle to Whipsnade in good time to get the feed mixed up and bottled for six. He recalls one morning being accosted by Police in a patrol car, who, eyeing him suspiciously, asked what he was doing out on his bicycle at that time of day! To which he replied, with his disarming smile 'I'm going to feed an elephant!' There really was no answer to that!

In those days, the staff cycled to work or travelled up and down on the Park's private bus. There were, however, days when the bus couldn't run and cycling was impossible because of the snow. Yet animal keepers, like shepherds and stockmen, must get through. Those are the very days when the animals depend on them most for their food, for ice on the water to be broken and extra bedding to keep them warm. Then the keepers simply have to walk. It is a long trudge up California Hill to be buffeted at the top by the furious snow being driven across the valley. The going gets harder – the snow settles against the Golf Club hedge and piles into deep drifts. If a car is trying

January snows, once a typical scene on the top of Dunstable Downs.   /BT

to make it through, and the driver offers a lift, one dare not accept – for, as John says, if the car ultimately gets stuck you feel obliged to give the driver a hand and that'll only make you later still ... They plod on, heads bent against the flurrying snow, boots heavier to pull out of the drifts with each step. There are no short cuts ... they follow the road ... there are too many dells - swiftly filling with snow - across the Downs. It's a long hard trek - followed by a long day of dragging food and bales of straw with freezing fingers and of breaking the thick ice on the ponds - and then, at the end of the day trudging homeward in the dark.

It was on one such day - January 1st 1962 - that Clive Bates started work at the Park. Fifteen years old and fresh from school - eager to start his first job - having to leg it through the early morning snow, with older, experienced men, who chivied him all the way - 'Keep up!' 'Get a move on!' 'We'll not be there on time!' 'What a start for you ... late on your first day!' It was hard going. He wasn't used to trekking three miles in deep snow so early in the morning. His heart thumped, not only with exertion, but with anxiety that he would be late and make a bad impression. But, once inside the Park, Lol Conway and his companions laughed - thumped him on the back and said 'Well done!' Years afterwards the glow he felt at their praises is still a vivid memory.

Clive Bates recalling his first journey to work through the January snows. In the background is all that is now left of the old Wolf Wood of my childhood.   /DP

❖ ❖ ❖ ❖ ❖

Work progressed throughout the Park - sinking fences into deep ditches to improve the panoramic view of the animals and, as the roads were widened for the flow of ever increasing traffic, the hedgerows were swept away. New picnic shelters and a new Rhino House and an enclosure for African rhinos were prepared. However, one major building replacement had not been planned.

One July evening, the Caretaker, John Forbes, who lived in the flat above the offices, was alone with his guard dog, Renny, when fire broke out. Alf Billington later told me that he and a friend were coming out of the Chequers Inn in the village, where they had spent the evening, when they were startled to see flames leaping into the sky from the direction of the Park. Making their way across the common to investigate, they saw that the whole of the Office building was ablaze. It will be remembered that it was a completely timbered structure, and to make matters worse the wood had recently been treated with preservative. Two workers from a firm of contractors, sleeping in a nearby hut, had rushed out and seized a ladder which they had pushed against the wall, hoping to rescue John through one of the upstairs windows. But the window was shattered and the inrush of air simply added to the conflagration. By the time the Fire Brigade arrived from Dunstable, there was no hope of saving either John or the building. He and his guard dog both perished ... The offices were completely destroyed.

One young keeper was sleeping in 'Continental Alley', the dormitory quarters in the Restaurant, so named because of the cosmopolitan mixture of staff who had slept there in the early days. Getting up next morning, he set out towards the Bird Sanctuary. Suddenly he stopped in his tracks and stared in total disbelief. The building which had stood in front of the Bird Sanctuary the night before, when he turned in, was no longer there. Barely a hundred yards away, despite all the noise and commotion, he had slept through it all!!

The smell of doused ashes pervaded the summer air as firemen picked their way through the debris trying to salvage valuable records. The thick, heavy scrapbooks of Press cuttings, which survived, still bear brown scorch marks on some of their pages, a reminder of the tragedy. From the ashes, phoenix-like, arose a new, modern building, with airy offices, a large conference room and two adjoining houses for senior members of staff. The architecture of the new building was in keeping with the new Entrance complex. They both symbolised the image of a Park which had to keep up with the times.

Between 1956 and 1967, the number of zoos in Britain had risen from twenty-odd to more than seventy and, in 1967, at least nine more were foreseen. Of all the Zoos created in the twenty-five years since 1942, half had been in Britain, which also accounted for a quarter of all

The office block fire. This fine wooden house had originally been built in 1932 for the Superintendent and his family. Since 1947 the entire ground floor had been used as offices and the upper floor had been converted into a flat. It was totally destroyed by fire on July 27th 1962. /DG

the new zoos worldwide. Besides all these new establishments, Whipsnade had to contend with the mushrooming Safari Parks. Its struggle for survival had started ...

As ever, Whipsnade's animals seemed to rise to the occasion. The sixties were heralded with the arrival of the second Great Indian rhino to be born in the Park – a bull calf called Manik. Then came the first twin polar bear cubs to be born and reared in captivity. As the Park swung through the sixties, two 'baby boom' years were recorded, among which were the first baby pygmy hippo, 'Podgy', and the first reindeer calf.

Sir Peter had written that Whipsnade had not had much success with reindeer, but this was about to be rectified. A female, transferred after being quarantined at Regent's Park, gave birth in May 1961. Perhaps, after the war, reindeer fared better by being fed on reindeer moss from Iceland. This was imported, dried and then soaked before being fed to the animals. In the late eighties, however, after the Chernobyl disaster, the moss was found to contain such high levels of radiation that its use was discontinued. Fortuitously, scientists have developed a pellet food which contains all the moss's valuable properties, a great blessing because, according to the keepers, reindeer moss was becoming far too expensive!

In December 1962, Frank Meakin's beloved tigress Kaseh, gave birth to a cub which was named Victor, after Frank's grandson. Unfortunately, Kaseh's milk dried up so Frank took the baby cub home the following tea time. His wife, Grace, welcomed the hungry little cub with open arms. She was only too happy to help hand-rear him, although bottle feeding would take at least half an hour, six times a day; after all she'd helped Frank rear Kaseh, some eight years previously, and what a beautiful loving animal she'd turned out to be. It's a pity tigers have such large claws – they'd make lovely pets – but their domestic cousins can wreak enough damage on furniture and human flesh with their tiny ones ... Grace watched with pride as the scrawny little frame filled out and Victor became a lively bouncing ball of fur, under her loving care ... he chased round their bungalow, playing hide and seek under the furniture and teased away at his favourite toy, a red mop. Bathtime was his great delight – tigers love water. Often Frank had broken the ice on the pond in the dell for Kaseh to bathe and watched admiringly as the beautiful creature stepped elegantly out of the water, shaking gleaming droplets from her gorgeously striped fur – a rich contrast against the snowy background. Now it was Victor's turn to go into the family bath. He watched eagerly as it was filled, plunging into the water at the first opportunity, trying to eat the frothy bubbles as Grace soaped him. Then, when thoroughly dried on a soft towel, the little fellow settled down to cat nap in front of the fire until Grace and Frank went off to bed. Trotting after them, he curled up on their feet. The next ten weeks of loving care passed all too quickly and the day came when he had to be returned to the Park.

Victor after he had returned to the Park.   */BP*

Frank Meakins had started work at Whipsnade three years before the opening ... In 1932, he had been one of the keepers accompanying Captain Beal to the station to receive the animals from Bostock's Menagerie, leading one of the camels back across the Downs ... later that year he had transferred to the Carnivores where, just after the war, he became Section Head Keeper and stayed in charge of the large animal Pits along the face of the Escarpment until his retirement in 1968. During those forty years he had overall responsibility for the breeding of thirty-nine tigers, nine lions, seven polar bears, two Snow leopards and four Kodiak bears – for which service he was awarded the Zoological Society of London's Bronze Medal.

One anecdote which illustrates this ruddy-complexioned man's humour happened in the days when meat was scarce. At that time the Society considered itself lucky to obtain consignments of condemned meat. Frank was conveying one such load of the green-dyed flesh, lobbing it over the bars with his pitchfork when a visitor remarked ... 'I say, my man, that meat's rather high, isn't it?' to which Frank with a twinkle in his bright blue eyes replied ... 'It has to be, otherwise I couldn't get it over the top!'

In November 1966, he welcomed Juanita, a cheetah, a sleek,

yellow, black-spotted, beautiful creature to his section, destined to become a legend in her own lifetime. There had been cheetahs in the Park in my childhood. Captain Beal told us tales of Rajahs and Princes riding out to hunt on the backs of their great elephants in beautifully decorated houdahs. Servants walked along beside them leading cheetahs, or 'Indian Hunting Dogs' as he called them, on leads or chains. Once the antelope were sighted the cheetahs were unleashed, lithely bounding off after them, their long legs swinging freely from their waists, their non-retractable claws serving them as a sprinter is helped by his spiked boots. For cheetahs, unlike other cats, do not stalk their prey, they run their quarry into the ground, achieving speeds of up to sixty miles per hour, making them the fastest animals on earth.

Cheetahs run with their long legs swinging freely from their waists.   */LM*

Not surprisingly, since they have a history of being handled, cheetahs can become quite tame. Frank often took a couple of them out on leads in the vicinity of the old Wolf Wood and the Children's Zoo. Perhaps his favourite was 'Edashera' which is Arabic for Eleven. Edashera had been the Regimental Mascot of the 11th King's African Rifles until they mutinied in 1964. As a result, they were disbanded and their mascot sent to Whipsnade. It wasn't long before his name was shortened to Eddie – after all Frank couldn't go round calling 'Edashera, Edashera' every time he wanted the handsome animal's attention!

Juanita was introduced to a fine male specimen called Jack, and within ten months of their first meeting gave birth to a litter of three cubs. This was an exciting event because, until then, cheetahs had been considered the most difficult of all the cats to breed in captivity. This was the first successful birth in this country and, probably, only the second recorded time that cubs born in captivity had been reared by their mother. The following July, Juanita and Jack produced a second litter. This was fortunate because by the autumn one of the first litter had died and the remaining two were in the hospital at Regent's Park, suffering from calcium deficiency. Juanita and Jack were to become legendary, in the zoological world, for their breeding, as you will read in the next chapter. Two African black rhinos proved to be another spectacular arrival. The black rhinos had suffered, not only at the hands of poachers but at the hands of those anxious to use the land where they lived for human habitation. They had become very rare now, but the Society had acquired two and they were brought to Whipsnade Park by the Director's son, Julian Tong. Having grown up in the Park and helped various keepers in his youth, Julian had taken himself off to Africa working for John Seago, an animal collector.

Juanita with her first three cubs.   */LM*

He came back again, three years later, this time with a wife *en route* for Canada, where he was taking up the post of Assistant Director at the Alberta Game Farm. Although it was his honeymoon voyage, he looked after a consignment of animals from Whipsnade, including a camel, several deer and a calf from the Ankole herd! In return the Canadians sent Whipsnade three Musk oxen. As their appearance suggests, these comparatively large animals, wild looking and shaggy, are related to both goats and oxen. Musk oxen roamed freely in Europe and Siberia in prehistoric times, but they are now only found in Canada and Greenland, where they are protected species. Their thick coats, which they need to guard against the intense cold, reach nearly to their feet and are so heavy that the animals can become almost exhausted by the weight if they have to journey long distances in search of food. Their horns curve outwards and upwards from low down on their faces, making them look for all the world as if they are wearing helmets. They must appear formidable when they make an outward-facing circle to protect their calves from predators. Before long, each of the females gave birth. The first calf was the first musk oxen to have been born in Britain since the Ice Age!

Two other species facing extinction arrived at Whipsnade at about this time. A pair of White rhinos from the Umfolozi Game Reserve in Africa and some European bison. It was, in fact, mainly Whipsnade's successful breeding of European bison, among others, that was to lead to its selection as a breeding ground for the White rhinos, in the seventies.

The European bison, or Wisent, once wandered all over the Continent but their numbers were much reduced by the eighteenth century. In the early part of this century and during the Great War, they were almost completely wiped out. After the 1914–1918 War an International Society had been set up to attempt to preserve what was left of the species. Lists were made of all beasts known to exist and a strict check was kept on breeding. Then the Second World War dealt them a further blow. By 1945 there were believed to be only some two hundred remaining in the Polish Forest of Biolowitza. In the 1960s the Polish Government had presented some of these to the British Forestry Commission. A bull and a cow were deposited at Regent's Park but it was felt that it would be a good move to send them, with their newly born calf, to join three females at Whipsnade to establish a herd.

The Park had had a herd of American bison since its inception. These are wild, humped cattle, which had roamed in millions over the grasslands and open woodlands of most of North America and Europe, but, alas, are now almost extinct in the wild. The American bison had been killed in huge numbers, partly to free land for farming and partly to deprive the native Red Indians of their main source of sustenance and survival, providing, as they did, food, clothing and even shelter. The original Whipsnade herd had consisted of seven bull calves, the gift of the Duke of Bedford. Females had been added, and I often enjoyed watching a newly born calf trotting behind its mother in their huge paddock alongside Bison Hill. The head and shoulders of this species are covered with thick, heavy fur, making them look more humped than their European cousins, which are, in fact, larger with more curved horns and longer tails.

At the same time that the Park was receiving endangered species, to play its part in their protection, two more pairs of Père David deer were taken back to China by Owen Chamberlain and Gerry Stanbridge.

During 1966, the second 'baby boom' year, perhaps the award for

A brown bear. /LM

the greatest stud achievements should have gone to Jacko, the Brown bear, who at about thirty-two was considered to be a good age. He had come from a circus in 1952 and he certainly hadn't lost any of his prowess or fatal attraction, for during 1966 he fathered eight cubs, with the co-operation of four different females! One gave birth to triplets, two to twins and the fourth to a single cub. The following January, when the gibbons were locked in their cage – lest they should escape across their frozen moat – the giraffes were kept in, for fear they would do the splits on the ice, and when extra root vegetables were put out for the wallabies, muntjacs and Chinese water deer as they were unable to graze, Nimrod, herself twenty years old, gave Jacko three more cubs. He was, indeed, a most prolific stud!!

By the end of that year nearly a quarter of the animals and birds in the Park were home bred, many hand-reared in the Children's Zoo, which was thriving in the hands of its capable hostesses. The only women attached to the keepering staff during the early years had been one or two employed to look after the Shetland ponies and lead them when they gave rides on summer afternoons. The replacement of the old Pet's Corner by the opening of a larger Children's Zoo, in 1954, had considerably widened the scope for women. Now, they were able to handle an even greater variety of animals as they hand-reared babies, including those of the more dangerous species, especially the bear cubs, which were fondled and petted by visitors to the Children's Zoo, until they were considered too old to be safe.

Most of the girls who did, and still do, hand rear the animals, took them home. Like Victor, they have to be fed at regular intervals, night as well as day. A young lady keeper could often be seen on a bus, with a wallaby poking its bright little head out of a bag. Linda Walker has since told me the girls depend a great deal on their parents' help when they want a night out. But that is something the parents of these 'animal mad' girls accept because,usually, the girl who comes to work at the Park has had a variety of pets of her own.

In the sixties, the main love of the girls in the Children's Zoo was horses and ponies and they all looked very smart in their old-style uniforms of jodhpurs and hacking jackets. They had no formal training, just picked up things as they went along from their more experienced colleagues, amassing what knowledge they could, knowing that they, in their turn, would be called upon to pass it on. The only requirements needed for the job were a neat appearance, a pleasing personality and an affinity for animals and people, especially children. It was not surprising that they didn't stay very long. With those qualifications they were soon married. During the winter months, they were able to ride the ponies, as we had done, but winter is not a time for slacking; there seems to be just as much to do as in the summer, when there are visitors to be entertained as well.

In 1966, however, one girl, Heather Holliday, had been allowed to leave the 'cloistered' confines of the Children's Zoo to work in the big wide Park. Heather had taken a Secretarial Course on leaving school, but, becoming 'mad about horses', she went to a local stables, where she met some of the girls from Whipsnade Park and decided to join them. After three years in the Children's section, she was moved out into the Main Park to look after birds, including cranes, geese and storks, and the sea lions. She said that the sea lions knew how to tell the time. One minute they were playing happily, the next they were straining anxiously in the direction from which the keeper would come with their food and, as I know from my own experience, they would call out to that keeper when he or she passed by. Heather lived for her work, dividing her time between it and caring for her invalid mother. It came as a great shock to everyone when she developed cancer and died in 1986 after twenty-five years at the Park, where she was the first woman to become a Senior Keeper. There is, very fittingly, a plaque to her memory in the Children's Zoo. She was, after all, a pioneer. Nowadays, women work alongside men in all the Sections.

The sixties saw some strange comings and goings. Whilst there was nothing strange about Mrs Ronald Biggs, the wife of the train robber, wanting to visit Whipsnade, her reason for doing so proved to be quite unusual. Driving into the Park, she was, by the ticket system then employed, able to prove that her time of arrival was two-thirty in the afternoon. This alibi proved that it was impossible for her to have been involved with her husband's escape from Wandsworth Prison at three o'clock on that day!

During this period, Whipsnade had its own escapee! Its wolf pack had become one of the largest in captivity and in 1965 one of its members decided to make a break for freedom. Sir Peter's early promise, to the local inhabitants, that the animals would not get out of the Park, had held well over the years, considering the vast numbers of creatures that have resided there since those first two wombats dug themselves out. One February day, the wolves were driven into a partitioned-off area of their wood for the Works Staff to carry out repairs to the fence in the main section. Suddenly one of the wolves made a spring for the fence ... clawing at the top of it, he scrambled over, leaped down, and headed off towards the boundary fence, pursued by some of the staff. No one actually saw him go over the boundary fence ... it was assumed that he'd taken off from an old tree root and made for Studham, so the Police were informed. Of course, there are always rumours ... vivid pictures, far larger than the realities of life, are painted. I have been told that a nameless someone told a nameless someone that he saw the wolf leap onto the back of a longhorn cow in a nearby grazing herd and propel himself over the boundary fence! There were, supposedly, hordes of policemen and tracker dogs out on the wolf hunt, although Owen Chamberlain, who followed it through to the bitter end, only saw about a dozen police at any one time and, although he has no doubt trackers dogs were used, he didn't see any.

All the staff that could be spared joined in the hunt. There were reported sightings from far and wide, but, at last, Owen Chamberlain and Victor Manton received one in time to pick up the wolf's trail. Before long they caught sight of it some fifty yards ahead, running across open fields. They followed at a good pace for several miles, the animal always managing to keep some fifty to a hundred yards in front. Their hope was to drive it into some sort of cover where they would be able to catch it alive in the nets they were carrying. At long last, a small wood came into view. With bated breath they waited for the wolf to run into it, but at that instant the spotter plane started to dive at the animal, which turned and ran off in the opposite direction, straight into a party of armed keepers who shot it. The wolf's three days of freedom were thus tragically ended.

Then there were the Army Cadets, destined to visit Ethiopia, who didn't know their animals! Apparently, stuffed ones had been placed strategically around their camp and they were sent out to find and identify them. The next step was to make contact with the real thing. No stuffed animals can be substitutes for live specimens, with their scents, movements and sounds. Where better could wild animals be

Owen Chamberlain telling me about the wolf's escape.   /DP

studied, in the open, than at Whipsnade.

Glider pilots, on the other hand, were unintentional visitors, only dropping in because they had crash-landed their aircraft. There have been many such mishaps. At one time the Gliding Club truck pulling its long narrow trailer was such a familiar sight that we simply shrugged and said 'Another glider down again'. Fortunately, they always missed the dangerous zones and although one pilot, at least, sustained back injuries, most of them walked away unscathed.

Some of the major construction work was put out to contractors. One of them employed an Irish labourer who habitually fried eggs on his shovel for his breakfast. One morning the keepers arrived at Spicers Field just in time to see him running for his life, full pelt across the field, pursued by the entire herd of Ankole and eland. With seconds to spare he scrambled up the wire fence, which bowed under his weight, and flung himself over the top to safety. Controlling their mirth at the spectacle, the keepers realised he'd been searching for mushrooms to add to his daily egg. My mouth waters at the memory of those mushrooms. I have seldom seen any to equal them for size and their flavour was out of this world. I loved it when my father took me with him mushrooming. Gingerly we climbed over the strong gate, whilst the zebra grazed placidly, shrouded in the early morning mist. The heavy dew soaked into our canvas shoes and chilled our bare feet as we cautiously criss-crossed the field, filling our brown paper carrier bag. Great was my mother's relief on our return. She was a nervous person as far as animals were concerned and dreaded even going to the village shop when Farmer Bates' cows were grazing on the Common. I wonder if the Irish labourer ever tried again and tasted those mushrooms himself?

Another Jacko came to Whipsnade. This one was a fine figure of a mynah bird, with black glossy wings and bright orange beak. He had been a family pet but for some reason or other they decided he needed

more company and brought him to the Park. His cage was placed beside one of the office windows, while it was decided what to do with him. He greeting everyone with a 'Good Morning' or 'Hallo' and said 'Goodbye' when they went out, a truly polite bird because he never, ever, swore. He loved company; as the typewriter keys clicked along he whistled an accompaniment, up and down the solfa scale. But, as someone with a keener ear than mine observed, he always left off 'doh'. No matter

A fine figure of a mynah bird. /BP

which way he went up or down the scale, he always omitted that last note. Eventually it was decided, no doubt with his best interests in mind, that he should be transferred to a larger cage out in the Park. Poor Jacko. He was unable to make the best of his new home. He'd hurt his wing and couldn't fly around his nice big cage. He sat, forlornly, on a solitary branch, day in day out. No doubt, he missed the noise and bustle, the comings and goings, the typewriters and telephones and the company of the two attractive girls Christa Datlen and Julia Timothy, whose space he had shared. He died soon afterwards; one wonders if it was from a broken heart?

Another sad little tale of this period is the story of Fifi, the hippo. Newspaper reports stated that the twenty-five year old Fifi had died at Belle Vue Zoo, Manchester, where she had been sent after killing her mate at Whipsnade! It sounded as though she had committed pre-meditated murder! Nothing could be further from the truth! For some reason, unlike most hippos, who are placid, gentle creatures, Fifi had a streak of wildness in her. Her keeper, Alf Billington, said he saw it in her eyes the day she arrived. It was borne out, by the windows she broke in her fury, in the teethmarks on the wooden doorpost where she sank them in her anger. But, he said, she never intended to kill Neville. It was a tragic accident caused by her temperamental nature. On the fateful day, Fifi was wallowing in their pond; Neville was inside. Suddenly, something startled her. In panic, she swept out of the water, rushed headlong to seek the safety of her house, just as the poor unsuspecting Neville was on his way out, plodding steadily down the slope. He was knocked off balance as she thundered past him and he crashed to the ground injuring his spine so badly that he never walked again. Surely a case of 'death by misadventure'. Fifi was subsequently

'She rushed headlong to seek the safety of her house.'   /BP

sent away. Not that that was an easy undertaking. She objected fiercely when it was time for her to leave. The keepers still recall the struggle they had trying to box her up for the journey; aggressive to the last, she kicked and kicked her crate, reducing its heavy timbers almost to matchwood! Neville and Fifi's premises were modified to provide a warm, indoor pool, so that pygmy hippos would be able to come to Whipsnade and remain all year round.

In 1967, the surrounding area was so badly hit by the worst outbreak of foot and mouth disease for fifteen years, that the Park was closed from mid November until the following mid February, only the second time in its history it had been closed, the other being at the beginning of the war. All but essential staff and vehicles were prohibited and the office staff had to wear wellington boots since footwear and vehicles were thoroughly disinfected before being allowed through the gates.

At about this time the Society was embarking on a programme which would widen the keepers' horizons. If Whipsnade was to keep up with the times, it was considered a good idea that some of the staff should be aware of what was happening on the Continent. Two trips were organised. The first was headed by Victor Manton, the Park's Veterinary Surgeon and Deputy Director, who took the group to Copenhagen, Cologne and Hamburg. The last of these must have seemed like a pilgrimage. It had been at Stellingen near Hamburg, that Karl Hagenbeck, son of a fishmonger, who had started a small menagerie trading in wild beasts, had established Zoological Gardens in 1899. He had pioneered a unique way of displaying animals out of doors, against scenic backgrounds, depicting their natural environments. Karl Hagenbeck's innovative ideas further fuelled by his visit to the Bronx Zoological Park in New York, had fired Peter Mitchell's imagination and prompted him to create Whipsnade Wild Animal Park, which was destined, in its turn, to become the prototype for Zoo Parks throughout the world. The second trip, led by Owen Chamberlain, now the Senior Overseer, visited Rotterdam and Amsterdam. Each member of the party gave up some of his annual leave and paid his own expenses. The recently retired Phil Bates accompanied the party, which included Lawrence Conway, David Longstaffe, Graham Lucas, Alan Morris, Jim Thorn and Harry Stevens, himself destined to make a memorable trip to South Africa in the not too distant future.

Ernest Tong retired in 1968. Various members of staff have said of him – 'He may have been a bit of a b****** at times, but at least you knew exactly where you were with him. He was the Boss!' The year after he left, there were over half a million visitors, as he had predicted. With his departure, the office of Director was abolished, his Deputy, Victor Manton, became Curator, and Owen Chamberlain took on the newly created post of Park Manager.

This was when Bob Wingate joined the keepering staff, full of enthusiasm to learn all he could. Bob was sent to the Bird Section and shortly after he started eight King penguins arrived to join the colony of Humboldt penguins already occupying the rock-strewn enclosure on the side of the Downs. Penguins are gregarious creatures. Some colonies in the wild can number more than a million birds. No doubt they believe in safety in numbers, for, as they search for food, they have to be very wary of predators. In spite of living so closely together in such large communities, they rub along peaceably for most of the time. They are only to be found in the Southern Hemisphere and it is said that the colder the areas in which they live the larger they grow. This seems to be borne out in the case of the Humboldts and the King penguins. The former, coming from the western coast of South America, are between fifteen and eighteen inches in height and the King penguin from Sub Antarctica is about half as big again. The little Humboldts are lively birds, busying themselves with swimming or waddling about their pen. They have speckles on their white chests and tinges of pink on their faces and at the ends of their flattish, broad, grey-black beaks. The statuesque King penguins are far less active, standing almost disdainfully by the edge of the pool, seemingly fully conscious of their 'majesty and magnificence'! Their 'shirt fronts' are white as the driven snow, with vivid patches of rich yellowish orange feathers at their throats and on either side of their dark heads. Shafts of deep rose pink run almost the entire length of the sides of their long beaks, which are finer and sharper than the Humboldt's, ending in evil-looking, downward points like sharp hooks.

The Head Keeper of the Bird Section gravely studied the splendid new arrivals and, sagely nodding his head, with clear authority announced that there were five males and three females! Young Bob was very impressed by this superior knowledge, because they all looked exactly alike to him! He asked for the finer points to look for, after all part of his chosen profession was going to be the sexing of these birds in the future! 'Ah, now, if I was to tell you that, you'd be as wise as I am!' came the reply! The new recruit was stunned! He'd been working in a Bird Garden and had joined the Zoological Society specifically to improve his knowledge and at his interview he had been told that he would receive the 'finest Zoological Training' in the world! Not surprisingly, he couldn't believe his ears; he went away and penned the following (with apologies to Longfellow):

Should you ask me whence these penguins,
Males and females how to sex them?
I should answer, 'I shan't tell you,
Lest you be as wise as I am.'

But, very soon, Bob was to get the training he had been promised. He was, in fact, one of the first group of keepers from Whipsnade to take the 'Keeper's Course' at Paddington Technical College. The Society had decided that, with the general public's ever increasing knowledge about wildlife, gleaned from excellent TV programmes, their keepers needed better training. The course was fairly comprehensive, both written and practical. Nowadays, one can be awarded a City & Guilds Certificate in Zoo Animal Management and this is an essential requirement if one wants to progress in this still somewhat out of the ordinary career. Not only, then, did Bob have the chance to train, but he, in his turn, was prepared to pass his knowledge on to others. Some years later, Penguin Biscuits held a national competition for the best essay on penguins. Bob went along to Studham School and told the children all about his charges at the Park, with the result that one of the children won a prize. Bob was invited back to make the presentation as a 'thank you' for his part in the child's success.

CHAPTER 9

Triumphs and Disasters
(the seventies)

In March 1970, Whipsnade learned that its success in breeding rare animals in captivity over the previous forty years was to be rewarded. At that time ten species were being preserved from extinction in the Park, including Père David's deer, Przewalski's Mongolian wild horses, pygmy hippos, musk oxen, European bison and both the Great Indian and African black rhinoceroses. Now the Chief Conservator in Natal decided that Whipsnade Park should become the European breeding ground for the White rhinoceros as well.

In olden times, these large, placid creatures, with their acute sense of hearing and smell, had grazed the entire length of Africa, from the Cape in the south to the upper reaches of the White Nile in the Sudan. Over the years, they had been under constant threat and harassment from humans, causing their numbers to dwindle, and the area they were able to occupy shrank to the land between the Black and White Umfolozi Rivers in Natal.

These rhinos have always fallen easy prey to human predators for, as I have said, they are, in the main, docile animals with poor eyesight living in great herds. They were known to the Ancient Greeks and were captured in Roman times and driven into the arenas for the games and amusement of the crowds. They have suffered horrendously at the hands of merciless poachers, seeking their horns. Not because they are ivory – rhino horns are, in fact, compressed hair – but none-the-less they are considered of great value, for legend says they have aphrodisiac properties. Ground into a fine powder and added to the desired one's drink, it is believed to be a powerful potion. This was still believed in the Middle East in the 1970s where the horn was fetching thousands of pounds. As well as being useful as a love potion, to own a dagger with a rhino horn handle was most desirable, as it was said to display the virulence and sexual prowess of its owner. With

White rhinos.   /BP

human vanity at stake, the poor creatures didn't really stand a chance. If only the poachers understood that rhino horns grow again. That, if they sedated the animals, they'd have a second crop in seven years.

After the Second World War, serious efforts had been made to tackle the poaching and had proved reasonably successful, particularly in the Zululand Game Reserve at Umfolozi. Twenty-five years after the war the White rhinos were so much on the increase in their native land that they were being distributed to Zoos throughout the world for breeding purposes.

There *had* been White rhinos at Whipsnade. The first huge male, Mash-a-Beni, was reckoned to be the most wicked animal his keepers had encountered. So much so that he is still remembered after all these years. No one was particularly sorry when he died and was replaced by another male, Moqunyana, whose name meant 'large eyes'; a fine specimen, standing six feet high at his shoulders and weighing about three tons (about as much as three family cars). He was accompanied by a delightful female, Ukhuko. However, since rhinos are gregarious creatures, it was decided that one large European herd should be established initially and Whipsnade was chosen as the venue, having unlimited space, with acres of, as yet, undeveloped land. A large expanse of the old agricultural area, at the Studham end of the Park, was prepared and landscaped for its new arrivals and Victor Manton, the Curator, and Head Keeper, Harry Stevens, went out to Natal to collect them. Since the Curator was to spend some time at the Game Reserve, it fell to the Head Keeper's lot to bring the animals home. He travelled with them to Durban, where they were loaded onto the Union

Harry Stevens with a litter of husky pups.

Castle ship, Kinnaird Castle, eight crates on the poop deck and the remaining twelve on the boat deck. Before long, it became very clear to the Captain that he had a problem. Since a rhino relieves itself of a wheelbarrow full of dung daily, and as there were seven bulls and thirteen cows on board, something would have to be done about the sanitary arrangements. The smell was already becoming unbearable. Fortunately, the crates had been designed to open at the ends for food and water to be put in for the animals. It was decided that, since the food was pushed in at one end, the dung could, just as easily, be pushed out at the other end, straight into the sea. Harry dealt with one side of the ship, John, his assistant, with the other. All went well, until

Harry developed a poisoned finger. Fortunately, again, help was at hand. A young Zulu seaman volunteered to take over Harry's side of the ship! The sailor was bewitched by one tiny female rhino, almost too small to have been taken away from her mother. She was his joy from day to day, happily receiving the affection he bestowed upon her, which no doubt compensated for the increased efforts he had to put into his 'labour of love' as they drew nearer to the Equator! As Harry Stevens said, 'He and John kept the Kinnaird Castle sweet smelling, whilst my finger steadily used up her medical supplies.'

The medical supplies were replenished in the Canaries and the ship sailed on to another unforeseen crisis. She was due to be in Cadiz, for several days, where the harbour is in the town itself. So the dung could no longer be pushed into the water! They didn't know what to do with the increasing mountain, until someone said they'd managed to find a local man who said he'd take it all away. They waited somewhat optimistically, only to have their hopes dashed when a little man popped up on the quayside with a very small donkey and cart! The first load made little impression. Completely undeterred, however, he came back next morning with a lorry. He beavered away, filling it, driving off and then coming back for more, with a huge grin on his face, completely disregarding the smell, the heat and the flies. Once having reduced the pile, he managed to keep the waste disposal under control for the rest of their stay. Harry Stevens said they just couldn't believe the good humour of the man and were completely flabbergasted when, at the time of settling up for his services, he refused all payment. Who knows? Perhaps the local wine was improved out of all recognition? 'White Rhino Vintage 1970'?!!

So they left their Spanish benefactor and the heat of Cadiz and before long were sailing up a fogbound Channel on their way to an England that had been bedevilled by dock strikes throughout the summer. At one point during the strike Whipsnade was reduced to one week's supply of fruit and another time Regent's Park had only a fortnight's supply of imported foodstuff. By July 16th the Government had declared a State of Emergency. Then, on July 22nd, the Union leaders agreed to recommend to their members that they unload perishable foodstuffs and cargoes in danger of deterioration. When I asked Vince Curzon if the Society had been concerned about the fate of the rhinos, he said 'No, they were sure that the dockers' humanity would prevail, as the animals had been on board ship for several weeks'. In the event, the dock strike was called off at the end of July, just days before the Kinnaird Castle docked in the Port of London, where heavy goods lorries drew up to carry two crated rhinos apiece along the motorway to Bedfordshire.

Everyone waited expectantly - Whipsnade already had a pair of Great Indian rhinos and a pair of African Black - these new arrivals would complete the set! There was also, although no one knew it that morning, to be an irony about their destinies! They arrived at about one o'clock in the afternoon - I was living on Tyneside at the time and how I wish I could have been there to witness what must surely have been the most impressive arrival of animals since Bostock's Menagerie in 1932.

The vehicles rumbled off down Central Avenue, through the Park, until they reached the new Paddock beyond the Children's Zoo. The crates were hoisted off the lorry by crane and set out in a line on the grass. Then each one was opened. The onlookers waited expectantly. At first, nothing happened. The animals had been in their boxes for upwards of six weeks; at last realising that the crates were open, sensing that there was something beyond, they nosed out slowly. Then, sniffing and snorting, they ambled off round the perimeter of their new field, marking out their territory. Owen Chamberlain has said, it was for all the world as though they were 'beating the bounds' of their new Parish! Once familiar with their new environment, they settled down to the very serious business of once more grazing off fresh sweet grass.

Vince Curzon was a young keeper on the rhino section at the time. Filled with excitement about the new arrivals, longing to see how they'd settled, he got up just before three o'clock in the morning the following day and set off for the Paddock, riding slowly on his motorbike over the damp grass in the half light of that August morning. As Vince surveyed the herd from the saddle of his motorbike he realised that they had split themselves up into pairs. In fact, he says, those friendship pairs he saw established that morning were to endure for many years. As

Vince Curzon   /DP

there were so many of them they were given numbers at first. Two females, fourteen and sixteen, later separated when they calved, rejoined each other immediately they were back in the herd. He said he was very sad when thirteen and eighteen were parted, one being sent to South America and the other to Asia. He had hoped they would have been kept together. But the most unlikely pairing of the morning was that of a large mature male and the little female that the Zulu seaman had been so fond of on the voyage. Malunda, the male, had suffered on his journey, his fine huge horn having been knocked off in his crate. No doubt, says Vince, he was feeling very sorry for himself. Little Katie had been taken away from her mother. She had found affection on the voyage. Now she was feeling lost again and was looking for a big, strong rhino who would comfort her. Katie and Malunda became inseparable.

Rhinos are, together with the tapir and the horse, the only surviving odd-toed animals. Besides having a completely different leg balance from all other animals, they neither chew the cud, nor do they have horns. Rhino horns, and White rhino bear two, the lower of which can grow very long, are, as I have mentioned before, made of compressed hair. White rhinos appear to be more 'streamlined' and longer-legged than their 'tank-like' Great Indian cousins. When I first looked across the expanse of grass and saw the fine herd of magnificent beasts, I wondered if some traveller in ancient times, seeing these greyish-white creatures with the long protruding horns, veiled in the African mist, had mistaken them for horned horses, giving rise to the legend of the Unicorn?

Only one of the herd had not come from the reserve – a big male, Gingindlhuva had been in a zoo. He was rather a solitary animal and went on to become the head of the herd. One female died soon after arrival. It was found she had come with blood poisoning. Monqunyana and Ukhuko were integrated happily becoming numbers twenty-one and twenty-two. Number nineteen had been pregnant on arrival and the year following gave birth to Whipsnade's first baby White rhino, a few months after Kidogo, the Black rhinoceros, had presented the Park with its first Black rhino calf, Kijana Nanyuki.

The White rhinos settled in and by the mid seventies breeding was well established. Then, one morning, disaster struck. Going to the Paddock first thing, one of the keepers found Katie lying on the grass in great distress beside her beloved Malunda, who seemed to be in the throes of a heart attack. Shocked at what he saw he rushed off to find the vet. They hurried back to the Paddock, but there was nothing they could do to save Malunda. Katie, they discovered, had terrible back injuries. It seemed that Malunda's little friend had reached maturity and he had wanted to take their relationship beyond the platonic. In trying to mount the little animal he had suffered the heart attack and in being forced to take the great weight of his body Katie's back had been broken and she died soon after.

Shortly after this Manik, the Great Indian rhino, who had been born in the Park and was one of its most valuable animals, was taken ill. He lay on the ground refusing to get up. The Veterinary Surgeon examined him and found a foot infection which was duly treated, but still Manik refused to get up. This was a very worrying situation, for rhinos lose the will to live if they cannot get onto their feet. After several days it was decided that drastic measures must be taken and the Fire Brigade was asked to help. They spent the entire afternoon trying to raise Manik with inflatable bags; doggedly, he refused to be helped.

His death was a great blow. There were, at that time, only some forty Great Indian rhinos in captivity, of which he was the only male in Britain. To make matters worse, the Society had, not so long since, purchased a female, Roopa, from the Delhi Zoo. She had suffered considerably on her journey by being confined in a crate that wasn't big enough for her. Vince Curzon says it is still possible to see the scars on her hide. She was so young he fed her by hand for several months after arrival. Then, just as she was reaching maturity, Manik had died. Great Indian rhinos were very rare and consequently very expensive; the Society could not afford a replacement. However, this story has a happy ending; Amsterdam Zoo came to the rescue, offering the loan of a male until Roopa had bred. In return Regent's Park sent a female to Holland. Four year old Kumar, who had been born in Berlin, arrived at Whipsnade in 1976.

The first calf of the alliance, a female, was born dead. The second, Bheema, later to be sent to Amsterdam as a replacement for his father, was born in March 1983. The Black rhino had calved the previous summer and a birth in the White rhino herd completed the trio. It was thought to be the first time that there had been young of all three species, at the same time, in any animal collection.

The Black rhinos were to be transferred to Regent's Park in 1988. Kumar stayed with Roopa, their latest calf, Bardia, being born in October 1989. The White rhinos went from strength to strength. There is no doubt that Whipsnade did its best to make them feel at home by calling the railway, which ran through their Paddock, 'Umfolozi', after their homeland. A privately owned company of enthusiasts had reached a two year agreement with the Society to run a two foot six inch gauge railway through the undeveloped part of the Park, between the Children's Zoo and this Paddock. So popular did the line prove that, within three years, it was extended into a complete circuit, cutting right across the area where the rhinos grazed. In fact, they were to cause so much damage to the engines that eventually, in the eighties, they changed places with the Asian exhibition, being moved to Spicers Field, which became 'Africa' as it always had been in my mind. Since the Umfolozi train couldn't very well run through Asia, it is now known as the Great Whipsnade Railway.

The Umfolozi, now the Great Whipsnade Railway, gets steam up.　　　　*/DP*

A Water Mammal Exhibition was developed in this part of the Park on the lower slopes of the old Home Paddock, where the gentle sweeping curves of its grey roof blend softly with the foliage of the surrounding trees. It consists of three separate water areas. An outer pool some sixty-two feet in length of shimmering, intensely blue water surrounded by viewing terraces on three sides. The inner, training pool and winter quarters is about twenty feet shorter, with seating for the public limited to some two hundred places on wooden benches on one side. Beyond this is a holding area or catch-up pool. It is possible to see the animals swimming underwater from an underground corridor running the entire length of the inner pool, through large one and a half inch thick plate glass windows.

In preparation for their new charges the keepers were trained by Sub Aqua Club instructors in the art of under water swimming in wet suits carrying oxygen cylinders. This meant that they were ready to deal with any emergencies that might arise as well as keeping the pool spotless. A very high standard of hygiene was required for the keeping of dolphins. So much so, that although now the dolphins have been replaced by sea lions, this has never been relaxed. According to Jane Pardoe, the Overseers frequently tell them that they have the cleanest sink in England and she says the brass scales on which they weigh out the fish, gleam. A far cry from the old galvanised bucket from which Alec was fed his fish, or the shed in the Works' Yard where it was prepared.

The Dolphinarium was to be the last major development in the Park for many years. The extension to the railway had meant the construction of a tunnel under Cut Throat Hill and the convergence of Cut Throat and Central Avenue was grassed over. Cars were diverted round Woodfield Paddock and a level crossing was installed by the station. Work went ahead on road extensions and a one-way system was introduced for busy days. By 1973 car admissions had increased by fifteen thousand since the mid-sixties. But within two years of the completion of this work the number of visitors was to fall by a sixth.

It had been hoped to establish an Arctic Exhibition for the polar bears, with a lake and foreshore with scree, but these plans had to be

The Dolphinarium, the last major development in the Park for many years.   */DP*

abandoned in the economic climate of the day and work concentrated on improving the breeding facilities and appearance of the old concrete structure on the Downs. At least when it was smartened up some thought it blended into the landscape better than it had done before.

A dolphin. /LM

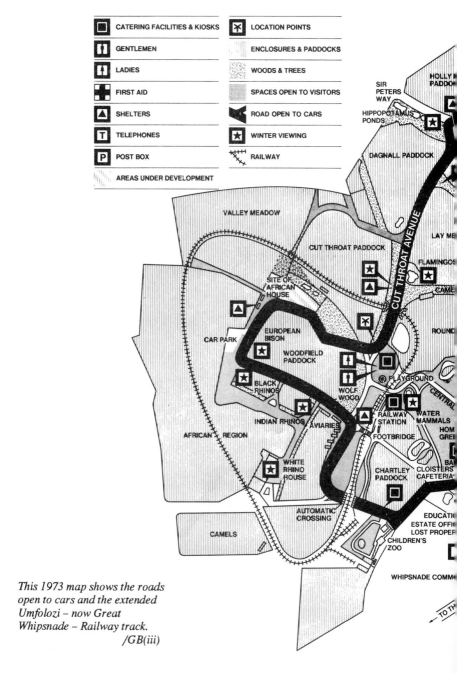

This 1973 map shows the roads open to cars and the extended Umfolozi – now Great Whipsnade – Railway track.
/GB(iii)

At any rate the bears bred successfully, having reared some nine cubs by the end of the seventies.

But now the Society faced serious financial difficulties. The number of visitors fell due to rival attractions and the increase of menageries in particular. Then zoos all over the country were forced by the Chancellor to charge eight percent VAT on all admission fees, something Whipsnade could ill afford to do.

Firstly the Dock Strikes had caused food shortages. Then inflation raged. Prices rose. In 1974 the food bill for eleven months was eleven thousand pounds more than it had been for the whole of 1973. By 1976 it was way over eighty thousand pounds and still rising. Hay went up by sixty pounds to one hundred pounds a ton. The elephants needed two tons a week, the White rhinos half a ton a day. Yet, in spite of all this, during those years the illnesses of the inhabitants were cut by seventy-five percent due to improvement in diet and feeding. Even the possibility of farming the red deer to help the finances was considered but proved unviable. Usually surplus animals were passed on to other menageries, a few being culled to balance the herds and provide fresh meat for the carnivores. Now other establishments were struggling to cope too and couldn't take them. The numbers normally put down had to be exceeded. The National Zoo Association of Great Britain offered to buy some of the animals which would otherwise have been slaughtered from their sixty member zoos and pay for their food. Six zoos closed, including the famous Belle Vue, Manchester, which had opened in 1836, only seven years after Regent's Park.

To make matters worse, the salary structure of the Zoological Society was revised. The salaries of the Scientific staff were pegged to University rates and those of the others brought into line with jobs in Local Government. The Society was forced to meet all these changes with none of the help from the Treasury which the Universities and Councils received. The wages bill made up forty percent of its total budget.

Then part of the Elephant House roof fell in and it was discovered that the glass domes of the 1930s were no longer safe. They were replaced by fibre glass at a cost of several thousand pounds. The house was sandblasted as well, which it was hoped would make it easier for the keepers to clean. By then Mangal Peary, the last of the riding elephants, was dead. She had been at Whipsnade for forty years. Jumbo, a young bull about nine years old, arrived from the Cameroons, having been presented to the Queen, who deposited him with the Zoological Society. He later turned out to be a very great problem indeed. Meanwhile, M'Tendre, the 'Peaceful One', one of the babies rescued in Zambia in the sixties was sent to Edinburgh.

Regionalisation of the herd animals continued. A fire in the Asian House damaged half the building and, although no animals were hurt, over two hundred tons of hay, most of which had been home harvested, was destroyed.

Lastly came a series of thefts. In the sixties, the office safe had been blown open and the weekend's takings stolen. Now the quarry was eggs and birds. When the first batch of eggs disappeared, the crows were blamed, but, one Sunday morning, the keepers found King penguin eggs missing. King penguins are good parents. They keep their eggs between their feet, protected by a fold of skin, until they hatch. Only a human being could have climbed over the fence and wrenched the eggs from the parent birds. On the other side of the Park, flamingo Keepers discovered nests, on which the birds had been sitting when left the night before, now bereft of their eggs. The Rosy flamingoes had refused to breed, until the Keepers had shown them the

King penguins are good parents.　/LM

way by manufacturing nests from a mixture of straw and concrete, hardened and daubed with clay. That, and an increase in the size of the flock, had led to nest building and egg laying. Now these eggs were gone.

Peace and tranquility, the Flamingo Pool.   */GS*

The robbers must have pushed the birds off their nests and snatched their eggs. The next theft of eggs, emu, rhea, ostrich and Manchurian crane, were taken from a display cabinet in the Children's Zoo. It was thought they were stolen to be sold, illegally, on the Black Market, where they would have been worth some two thousand pounds. Then, the following autumn, a man was gaoled for stealing two Snowy owls and a macaw. After that, a white cockatoo, a mynah bird call Rajah, two pheasant chicks and a rare gosling went. Eventually, there was a phone call from Tring. The white cockatoo had been found.

Gerry Stanbridge and Bob Wingate drove over to collect it. They found the bird bent on pecking its way out of a cardboard box. 'How did you get it in there?' they asked, knowing full well that the bird's beak was strong enough to peck a finger off! 'I just put it in!' the man who had caught the bird replied. Which, as Bob says, was truly a case of 'Where ignorance is bliss'. This reminds me of a story Pete Williams tells. After eighteen years at Regent's Park, he decided to move to Whipsnade, something no one in London could understand. He says, he began to wonder himself as he travelled across the Downs on the Park Staff bus to report for work in a blinding snow storm on All Fools' Day! Shortly after his arrival, he was in the Children's Zoo when he noticed a Keeper piling on layers of clothes. 'What's all that for?' Pete asked as the man pulled on another pair of gloves. 'I'm going to pick up that bear cub,' came the gruff reply. No sooner were the words out of his mouth, than a young girl hostess swept past them, shirt sleeves rolled up, gathered the cub in her bare arms and made off with it!

Nothing was ever heard of the fate of the gosling and the chicks, but, some days later, word went out that Rajah, the mynah, was perched in a tree behind the Estate Office. Perhaps his strong language, dirty jokes and wolf whistles – he was not a polite bird like that other mynah, Jacko – had been too much for his captors. Maybe they'd decided that there was no market for a bird with his repertoire and had set him free! Bob was given the job of catching him. It was one of those miserable days when the rain drips off the trees and runs down your neck as you walk beneath them. Bob peered up at the bedraggled bird. It was no good, he'd have to climb up after it. Everyone watched as he struggled on the slippery bark, dousing himself as his cold fingers sought to get a grip on a branch, slithering, sliding, matters only made worse by the bird staring down at him, with its beady black eyes and repeating constantly 'What's the matter then?'

I recalled Graham Lucas's similar exploit, climbing a tree to bring a cheetah down, one hand supporting its rump, the other immobilising it by gripping the scruff of its neck, in the same way as one immobilises a pet cat, but in his case, leaving no hand free to hold the ladder! He also tells a tale about the instruction of a young Trainee Keeper on 'Safety in the Cage'! Following his Head of Section, the lad watched as the older man swung open the gate of the pen and marched in. Two paces and the Keeper caught sight of the angry swish of a leopard's tail, hanging down from its platform, and stepped back even more smartly than he'd stepped in, slamming the gate smartly shut! Turning to the Trainee, he asked brusquely, 'Well, did you see my deliberate mistake then?' 'No,' the lad shook his head. 'Always check the cage first to make sure it's empty. Now I've shown you the wrong way I'll show you the right.' The Keeper called the leopard into its house and shut the door. 'When you've done that, then you go in!', he added, feeling sure he'd saved face.

Graham himself, was part of the 'Big Cat' section during its great triumph. There were times when the seventies were lean and disappointing, but 'There is a tide in the affairs of men!' which led to a fortune for the Whipsnade Wild Animal Park and which resounded around the entire zoological world.

As I've already said, a four year old female cheetah, Juanita, arrived at the Park in 1966. Having been introduced to ten year old Jack, who had come from the Nairobi National Park a couple of years earlier, she produced a litter of cubs the following September. They had been the first cheetah cubs bred in this country and were believed to be only the second litter ever reared in captivity! She and Jack continued to breed and a second record was achieved when their daughter, Janica, had cubs. For they were the very first second-generation cheetah cubs to be born in captivity. Movement was now possible between menageries for breeding purposes. Juanita and Jack's first male cub, Frank, was sent to Jersey. During the seventies twelve of their progeny were sent to other British zoos and twenty-six distributed world wide to places as far apart as Jersey and Jerusalem, Sydney and Durban and Wellington and Edinburgh.

Then, in March 1977, Jack died from a pox virus. Juanita was moved to Regent's Park, where, the following September, ten years to the month after giving birth to her first cubs and to a legend, she too died. For it is acknowledged that Juanita and Jack were the greatest pair of breeding cheetahs that zoologists have known. From that initial alliance, one hundred and twenty nine kittens have been born in thirty eight litters and into the fourth generation.

So Whipsnade had every reason to celebrate the seventies, which had started with the arrival of the twenty-strong White rhino herd and ended with the return of a Common hippopotamus to Africa. Winnie, the grand-daughter of the Park's oldest inhabitants, Henry and Belinda, was sent to Swaziland to become the mate of a solitary member of her species, in a Wild Life Sanctuary.

Never mind the cheetahs, what about the keepers? Three generations of Bert Rogers' family have clocked up some 112 years at Whipsnade between them.

Bert, it will be recalled, had worked on Hall Farm before it became a Zoological Park. In 1934 with the arrival of the giraffes, he joined that section and stayed with these beautiful animals until his retirement in 1958. He was also responsible for the pair of Indian rhinos. In 1936 together with the pair of Baringo giraffes, they were the most valuable animals in the Park. On Boxing Day the following year, Rosie gave birth to Whipsnade's first baby giraffe. Many more calves followed this initial success, earning Bert the Zoological Society of London's Bronze Medal in the early fifties. Then the year before he retired, the Indian rhino produced their first calf.   /MW

Leading the camel, the author and little Rebecca on top, is Gerry Stanbridge, who married Bert's older daughter Elsie; Gerry came to the park in March 1947 and stayed until his retirement some forty years later. As the Senior Overseer, he accompanied Owen Chamberlain to China in 1973 to return some Père David deer to their native land. /GS

Andy White married Gerry's daughter Maureen. A mechanic, he visited the Park after a motorcycle accident and decided to stay. Andy, Overseer of the Asian Area, has been at Whipsnade for almost thirty years and his wife has served in the Gift Shop for thirteen years. /DP

CHAPTER 10

Golden Jubilee and the Eighties

On Saturday 23rd May 1981, fifty years to the day since first opening to the general public, the gates of Whipsnade Park swung wide to the pealing of the bells of the church of St Mary Magdalene. It was the first time in the history of the church on the hill that six bells were rung.

The Church of St Mary Magdalene, Whipsnade.   /DP

Until then, there had been only three, one of which was cracked; now, with the old ones re-cast and three new, smaller ones added, they rang a celebration peal for almost two and a half hours to celebrate the Golden Jubilee of the Wild Animal Park which had made the little village's name famous throughout the world. Visitors on arrival found it to be a truly 'thirties' day as they paid the same price for admission as the first people had paid, fifty years before; Adults 1/- (five pence), Children 6d (two and a half pence). Cars were not allowed in, but ample free car parking was available outside. Vintage buses ran visitors round the Park which was now home to nearly two thousand animals of some one hundred and eighty two species, over eighty percent of the animals and fifty percent of the birds being 'home bred'.

For the first time since the early 1950s the famous Whipsnade White Lion was lit up. This time there were seven hundred and fifty high-powered white bulbs and the lighting equipment was the gift of Hadyn International Ltd. People who have, obviously, no idea of the amount of work which has to be put into the upkeep of these chalk figures, frequently complain to the local press about the dingy state of the Lion. We shall actually never know how many of these figures have been lost throughout the land, due to neglect, as grass and weeds have encroached on them. I once read that the Cerne Abbas Giant which is one hundred and eighty feet in length, and the Long Man of Wilmington, two hundred and twenty-six feet, both need weeding annually. The Lion of Whipsnade is much larger than either of these, being four hundred and eighty feet from nose to tail. The Zoological Society has always relied very heavily on voluntary help to maintain it – Scouts and Cub Scouts in 'Bob a Job' weeks, 18 Plus and Young Farmers Clubs. Perhaps, instead of picking up a pen, 'would be' critics could serve a more useful purpose by taking up the trowel! After all, it is a local landmark, as well as Whipsnade's symbol, and its image is used as the logo of South Beds District Council. In Jubilee Year, however, the Royal Navy lent a hand. One would hardly expect to find sailors cleaning a chalk lion on the side of the Chilterns, but these young men on an Electrical Engineering Course on HMS Daedulus were allowed to undertake a completely different project for one week

Many times in the past visitors asked the way to the 'white lion' and were very surprised to find out it wasn't a real animal but a chalk lion.   /GS

each year. At various times a number of such groups had come to Whipsnade. One contingent extended the pond in Round Close which was known, ever after, as Lake Daedulus in deference to the men who made it. On another occasion they repaired the vultures' cage when it was blown down in a gale. Now, they were assigned to the White Lion with eighty tons of whitening chalk, a powder used in paper production, which had been donated by Blue Circle Industries. It is, invariably, breezy on the Downs and Owen Chamberlain still laughs as he remembers the sailors coming along Duke's Avenue, at the end of their day's work, covered from head to foot in white powder. 'They looked like the flour graders in the television advert', he says.

The Duke of Edinburgh, who had been the President of the Zoological Society of London from 1960 until 1977, arrived to launch the celebrations. He was greeted by the Lord Lieutenant of Bedfordshire, Lt. Col. Hamner Hanbury, Whipsnade's Curator, Victor Manton, and the President of the Society, Lord Zuckerman, who, as a young scientist, had come to Whipsnade for the first time on Sir Peter's picnic. In his after luncheon speech to the special guests, the Duke said Whipsnade's 50th Anniversary was a fine achievement, and he congratulated the staff for keeping the Park in such magnificent condition. He said that he hoped it would go on for another fifty years, but, whatever the future held, it had a marvellous record to look back

The Duke of Edinburgh at the Golden Jubilee celebrations with children from Studham School.   /DG

on. How proud Sir Peter would have been! Captain Beal was also dead by then, but Mrs Beal was at the party. My father should have been, but was in hospital following an accident. Sadly, he died two weeks later. Seventy-eight year old Phil Bates, however, was there to celebrate.

The Duke visited a Wildlife Conservation Exhibition in a marquee on Hall Farm Lawn, a Photographic Exhibition showing the development of Whipsnade and its animals, in the Hall Farm Aviary, and he met Mrs Constance Benn, who had won a competition organised by the Luton and Dunstable Camera Club for the best picture taken in the Park. Then he toured the grounds on the road train and had a ride on the Umfolozi Railway, which had been inaugurated by Princess Margaret some eight years earlier, before ending his five hour stay at the Dolphinarium, where Sampson, Nina and Esther were put through their paces. Finally, he flew off in the Royal Helicopter. The only thing that had marred the day was the weather with its intermittent drizzle. But, as I wrote at the time, in an article in the Dunstable Gazette, Whipsnade has always been a golden place where a kind of glory shone through, even on the rainy days.

Other events during that 'Golden' summer included an Open Day for under privileged and handicapped children, special days for the Panda Club, the junior section of the World Wild Life Fund, and the XYZ Club, the Society's Club for children between the ages of nine and eighteen. Dunstable Round Table organised a Family Day, which, they said, wasn't a profit-making venture; they just wanted people to enjoy themselves! Souvenirs, car stickers, mugs, bookmarks and children's T-shirts were on sale throughout the season.

On a more serious note a Symposium on 'Advances in the Veterinary Care of Zoo Animals' was held at Regent's Park, in recognition of the experience and knowledge gained at Whipsnade, both as a breeding centre and in the conservation of wild animals. Its unique contribution to the Wild Life of the world, from its unrivalled experience in the management of captive animals, was acknowledged, as was its role in providing other collections with captive-bred animals, thus reducing the demand for animals to be taken from the wild. Apart from anything else, Whipsnade had proved that wild animals can survive in the open air in our climate, something of which many of its rivals were now taking advantage. Only the year before, a second generation chimpanzee, the first such to be born in any British zoo, was born in the Park. Its mother, Primrose, had been one of the London Zoo's 'Tea Party' chimps and its father was called Oscar.

There must be something in the Whipsnade air, because it is said that male chimps rarely reach maturity until nine years of age. Oscar was seven! Remember Tiny Tim?

Severe January weather followed the Jubilee year. Snow piled high against the fences. A Red panda climbed over and escaped. He was run to earth in Tring Road, Dunstable, where a dog owner thought his pet was chasing a fox, until the small ginger-coloured animal shot up a tree! Attendances declined by twelve percent, in spite of reduced prices for the first three months of the year. There was barely any money to purchase a companion for the recently bereaved dolphin, Samson.

He had happily shared the pool with Nina and Esther for almost six years, giving daily displays to delight the visitors. Then he finally succeeded in making Nina pregnant! Joan Crabtree – who applied for a job in the Park after seeing a TV programme about a zoo and was moved to the Dolphin Section once it was established she could swim! – recalls the birth of Nina's baby. It happened at lunchtime on a summer's day. Esther and Samson were locked away, leaving Nina alone in the pool. The staff, watching expectantly! from the observation window, saw a little tail emerge. Dolphins are born tail first, so that they can breathe inside their mother and not drown, because, although they are aquatic animals, they can drown if water gets into their lungs. Joan says it was all over so quickly. The little calf darted across the pool and banged its beak on the gate which separates the inner and outer pool, a blow which was to prove fatal. As the days passed, there was obviously something wrong with the baby's breathing. Then it began to sink and Nina made no attempt to help it rise up until, at last, it lay on the bottom of the pool. The keepers netted it out and it was found to be dead. A gloom descended upon that glistening corner of the Park. The post mortem revealed that the damage to the beak had passed along the baby's spinal column. After the loss of her baby Nina became anorexic, refusing all food. As the beautiful, gentle creature grew steadily weaker, it was decided that she would have to be force-fed. Donning wet suits, some of the staff slipped into the water and half lifted her on to the sling-like stretcher on which dolphins are transported. Once out of the water her tail was held to immobilise her. Joan shuddered as she told me what happened next … 'it was horrible, but necessary,' she said. Nina's mouth was forced open and her jaws held apart with towels, whilst fish were coaxed as far back in her throat as possible to make her swallow them. Sadly, force-feeding didn't save her life and Nina lived barely four weeks after her baby.

Then, Esther died from old age ... Samson was alone. Dolphins are gregarious creatures; no doubt missing his companions, he developed behavioural problems, the worst of which was banging his head violently against the glass observation window, cracking it in spite of its thickness. A short time after, a female called Lady was sent from Windsor Safari Park to keep him company.

Not long before the dolphin tragedies, Pole Pole, an elephant being moved from Regent's Park to Whipsnade, had also died. The dictum of the day was that elephants should not be handled; it was thought to be unnatural for them to have too much human contact! Not that Dixie or any other Zoo's riding elephants appeared to have suffered much through handling. In fact, they had all appeared to enjoy human contact. Perhaps, in some way, it made up for the family group they would have been with in the wild. At least, with something to do and people to fondle them, they were rarely bored. However, Pole Pole was bored and young, bored elephants develop vices and, even if they are female, become unmanageable. This had begun to happen to Pole Pole, with the result that she was losing condition. A change of surroundings with a transfer to Whipsnade seemed to be the answer, but she would need to be sedated for the journey. There were those who were concerned that if she were put to sleep, in her condition, she might be too weak to get back on her feet again. There was, in America, a new antidote, but as it was as yet untried in this country it was thought to be too risky to use! In the event, the animal was down for too long and died. How sad! When I think how happily Dixie trundled into the wagon that took her to the Film Studios, it was almost as if she enjoyed the ride. But then she'd been a travelling elephant all her life!

Pole Pole's death caused a great outcry. Discussion rocked back and forth between those for and against the keeping of wild animals. Various pressure groups were formed, including Zoo Check, whose declared aim was the phasing out of all zoos. They would have all animals in Reserves in the wild, leaving those who can never afford to go on safari trips to be content with stuffed specimens in museums, or fleeting television pictures in the corners of our sitting rooms. Forever deprived of the live sound, smell and, sometimes, even the feel of these creatures. The animals themselves, likely to disappear overnight, with the vagaries of the fortunes of their various homelands. Then, Greenpeace raised the question of the large numbers of dolphins and killer whales dying in captivity, and called for a ban on all imports. Within two years the Government announced new standards for the keeping of large sea mammals and asked all operators for immediate comments. As a result of the findings of the Klinowska Report, all imports were banned. Considering its pools to be inadequate and completely unable to find the twenty million pounds, or more, needed to create proper facilities for dolphins, Whipsnade despatched Samson to Spain and Lady to Morecambe, Lancashire, where, regretably, she subsequently died.

A Federation of the Zoological Gardens of Great Britain and Ireland, based in London, had been established as early as 1966. Its aims were to maintain standards in the care of housing, hygiene and transportation of animals and in public safety. All member zoos, of which Regent's Park and Whipsnade Wild Animal Park were Founder Members, were required to submit their premises for periodical inspection and to exchange ideas in zoo practice. The Federation would also give technical advice to Local Authorities on the opening of zoos. There had been instances of cruelty, where animals had been in cages too small for them, or had been injured by being left too long in poor conditions. The Federation also wanted zoos to provide educational facilities combined with places where scientists, vets and doctors could work, learning about animals. Whipsnade made plans for an Education Centre, with a separate entrance, but there wasn't enough money to carry out the work.

Richard Kock in shirtsleeves with John Datlen the Senior Overseer. /DP

By the mid-eighties, public interest in Wild Life had been aroused. There was a greater increase in visitors to zoos than in any other section of tourism in 1986, but many fell below acceptable standards. Problems were being tackled, but, as Richard Kock says, 'Progress was slow, something which, inevitably, gives rise to pressure groups, which can swing as far the other way, if not tempered.' 'However,' he added, 'when these groups criticise, one must think, is there anything they are saying which is true?' and he illustrates this with his delightful story of the 'Bald Polar Bears'.

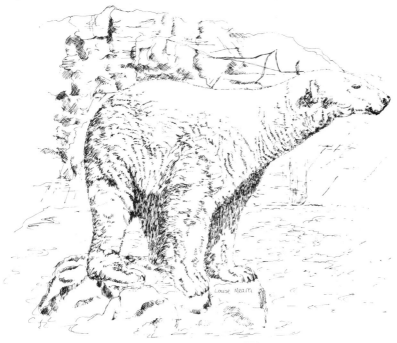

A Polar bear. /LM

One day, he came upon a man from Zoo Check, standing by the polar bear pen. 'These animals aren't happy', the man said. 'Oh!' Richard replied. 'No, they've got alopecia ... that's caused by stress, you know'. Now, Richard, who is perhaps the best zoologically qualified veterinary surgeon the Park has ever had, holding as he does a Degree in Wild Life Management among other academic achievements, knew only too well, that, contrary to some idealist's mode of thinking, all ailments are *not* due to psychological disorders; some are simply biological. He returned, thoughtfully, to his office. There was nothing wrong with the bears' appetites, they were eating very well. Nevertheless, he studied their diet sheets. Polar bears need a million units of vitamin 'A' per day, far more than human beings can possibly tolerate. That was it! They weren't getting enough vitamin 'A'. He contacted Roche Products, the pharmaceutical group, and they provided a powder, which was sprinkled, liberally, on the daily intake of food, with the result that the hair rapidly grew again and the bald patches disappeared! A few weeks later, the Zoo Check member paid another visit. 'Ah, I see you've changed the bears,' he said. 'No, just their diet,' Richard replied, but he had the greatest difficulty in persuading the man that it wasn't boredom but a lack of vitamin 'A' that had cause the problem.

From the point of view of the ungulates, Richard Kock couldn't have arrived at a better time, coming as he did at the very end of 1982. In order to eke out hay and grass, they were, like so many farm cattle at that time and since, being fed a dairy pellet supplement product. Pete Williams says it was strange to watch them when it was first introduced. Herd animals have a 'pecking order', and the male wasn't at all sure it was time for him to begin. Richard's first concern, however, was that most of these were not dairy cattle. He, therefore, made arrangements for BP to manufacture pellets to suit the special requirements of the different species. As a consequence, no offal went into these new diet supplements. No one will ever be able to measure the impact this change of food, at that particular time, had on the stock, but what it does mean is that none of the animals or home bred calves run any risk of contracting BSE, more commonly known as 'mad cow disease', which, if it had taken hold in the Park, would have meant total disaster for Whipsnade.

As a child, I used to be worried by the kinds of food given to some of the animals. Why did the elephants have hay and potatoes, I wondered, knowing full well how much they enjoyed the odd acorn? But the feeding of animals has changed beyond all recognition and long gone are the days when the bears were fed the stale cakes that the pastry cook had made and the Restaurant couldn't sell. I was talking to Andy White one day as Marilyn Sudder was taking provisions for the Care Centre from his Ford Transit which was well laden with, he told me, over one hundred pounds' worth of cabbages, carrots, tomatoes and other vegetables. For a few months, just over a year ago, he said, the Park had had a bonanza! The ASDA Supermarkets had a depot nearby and, their quality control being exceedingly high, anything that didn't measure up was given to the Park. Unfortunately, the depot was moved!

Animal food costs, in 1989, were £205,800. To ease the situation,

Marilyn Sudder with Tilly, a hand-reared wallaby.   /DP

fresh vegetables are dropped and pellet food increased at expensive periods and the process reversed as fresh supplies become cheaper. Food is increased in the winter when the animals have inclement weather to contend with. Except for the reindeer. Firstly, it seems, the reindeer moss wasn't as beneficial as was earlier believed, but neither were they doing very well on hay. As Richard points out, their bodies aren't geared to digest grass. They were still suffering a fairly high mortality rate. Then, he realised, their food was, like that of the other animals, being increased in the winter. Reindeer are not used to eating in the winter in their natural habitat. It is then that their food is scarcest. So, they put on weight in summer to combat the winter scarcity, like hibernating animals. Since the amount of summer feed has been increased, the herd has gone from strength to strength. Whipsnade's reindeer are a sight to behold in August!

By 1984, the Society hovered on the verge of bankruptcy. In an attempt to cut expenses, Whipsnade's exhibits were brought closer to the main roads to make them more convenient for the staff to deal with, and the range reduced in order to concentrate on specimens most in need of conservation. Help and funds were needed. Shades of the early miners returned when a YOP group of youngsters converted a little used shelter, in the Children's Zoo, into a house for tortoise

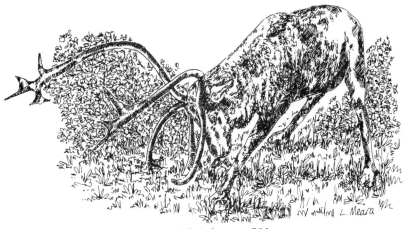

A Reindeer.   /LM

breeding, and another team under the Manpower Services Commission prepared the Asian House in Spicers Field. The Park became the venue for Sponsored Walks, plus a Round the World Conga Competition and it ran special events – Father's Day, Easter Egg Hunts and Visit Father Christmas. An Animal Adoption Scheme, first launched during World War II, was revived to help cover some of the feeding costs. It is still functioning, with both individuals and groups responding. Currently, it starts at fifteen pounds a year for a rabbit, guinea pig or a gerbil, rising to five hundred pounds for a yak and five thousand pounds for an African elephant. White rhinos and tigers cost two thousand pounds a year to keep.

The large, thick-coated Siberian tigers (of which there are less than four hundred in the wild) who had produced their first litter in 1982, produced another at the beginning of the Chinese Year of the Tiger! Perhaps an omen which foretold an unexpected windfall from the Middle East. The authorities in Qatar, in the Persian Gulf, were gravely concerned at the way in which visitors to the Doha Zoo were behaving badly, even throwing stones at the animals. They turned to the Zoological Society for help and a team from Regent's Park and Whipsnade, under the leadership of David Jones, set out to create a Park with better elements for the animals; although smaller, it had a Whipsnade feel about it. The Society contributed some animals and managed the Zoo for a time, in order to establish 'standards'. As a result of this consultancy, they received a fee which enabled the Park to have six new buildings – a Unit for Zoology – a new Giraffe House – and three new Antelope Houses – which were erected by contractors and fitted out by Whipsnade's Works staff. The new Giraffe House, on much the same lines as the 1930s one, was built behind the old one which was then removed.

The new Giraffe House.   /DP

Unfortunately, the first Ungulate House to be completed was half destroyed by a fire the same night, caused by a gas heater. Although prompt action by the staff, living on the premises, managed to save the rest of the building, a pregnant zebra, a young male Congo buffalo and a recently imported bontebok perished. A new House for the Greater flamingoes, with large plate glass windows for winter viewing, was built on the Chartley Paddock side of the Old Home Paddock and the flamingoes were moved from the Children's Zoo to a larger, beautifully-landscaped pond. All these new houses were tastefully set in their new surroundings and very well appointed, a stark contrast to the early wattle-sided sheds.

For some years, there had been concern about the inadequacy of the accommodation for the polar bears and, since money was now too tight to contemplate providing any alternative and the feed alone was costing some four thousand pounds a year, a new home was found for them at Chester Zoo. Their neighbours, the Kodiak bears, were sent to Duisberg some six months later. Although these huge bears had never been exhibited at their best, in the deep pit in which they had lived since 1947 they had, like the polar bears bred well. That same year

(1984), Paul, the Common hippo, was sent to Milwane Wild Life Sanctuary, to join his sister Winnie in a group of hippos which were managing to survive the relentless hunting of the poachers, seeking meat, sports trophies and ivory from their teeth. According to the High Commissioner, who launched an Appeal for help, he left in a crate which cost three thousand pounds.

Meanwhile, Jumbo, the bull elephant, had grown more and more unmanageable. At first, he had been a playful young elephant, but, by the time he was fourteen, he was, to use the words of his keeper Carla Tams, 'like a boisterous teenager'. Had he still been living in the wild, he would, by this time, have been in a bachelor herd. As it was, the other elephants, all females, bullied him. One of the young men keepers had been in the habit of romping with him, swinging on his large tusks, and pushing him playfully across the yard. Until, one day, Jumbo pushed back! Shoving the helpless lad over the bare ground he suddenly realised he was the stronger and from that moment Jumbo lost his respect for man! At musth, the time of sexual excitement in elephants, he changed from a placid animal into a regular nuisance,

Jumbo. /BP

pushing the keepers about with his strong trunk. Then, one day, he dropped the young man, his former 'playmate', to the ground like a sack ... it was very frightening, threatening. Instantly, Kumara, the only Asian elephant in the compound, moved across and stood over the keeper protectively. Ever after this episode, she would position herself between Jumbo and the keepers, somehow seeming to sense that she had a duty to look after them. Jumbo, on the other hand, became increasingly more wild and difficult to handle. Talking to me one day, Carla relived the nightmare of getting him into his stable. Ideally, it needed three keepers, one on the steps inside the house to entice Jumbo in, one inside the stable ready to slide the heavy curved door shut and the third by the barrier, on the visitors' side, acting as the door-keeper's 'look-out', shouting once the elephant was far enough inside for the door to be shut. It was always a nerve wracking few moments, particularly for the keeper on the door. One day, there was only Carla and a young girl Trainee keeper. All the elephants were at the top of the Paddock as they opened the gates and called them. Kumara obediently responded, leading the way, but Jumbo doubled back as soon as Carla shut her in her stable. Suddenly the Trainee

Kumara.
/BP

yelled 'Look out!' Turning, Carla saw Jumbo charging full pelt towards her. Instinctively, she swung herself through the bars of the compound, out of his reach as he bore down on her, thrusting his tusks through the barrier. In spite of this, he still had to be shut in for the night. The girls had to go back in the pen with him ... As the senior of the two, it fell to Carla's lot to climb back into the paddock and bait him back up the slope, while the Trainee slipped into the stable to man the door. Once her assistant was in position, Carla ran for the stable,

Jumbo chasing her; deftly, she stepped aside and he thundered past her into his stall. The younger keeper pushed the door to and just managed to escape, as the large animal turned, swinging his trunk, menacingly!

With Carla Tams in the elephant keepers' mess room.   */DP*

It became increasingly obvious that Jumbo was a danger to all those who had to handle him. Desperately, the Society tried to find a collection that would take him off their hands. At twenty-three, he was a fine specimen but there were no takers and, with no other option open to them, he had to be put down. It was a heartbreaking decision but necessary to prevent the very real possibility of a human fatality. Soon after this, Kumara was sent to join the elephant herd at Chester Zoo, in the hope that she will successfully breed there.

What a pity that, with all its space, Whipsnade cannot have a breeding herd. M'Tendre, by now a solitary animal in Edinburgh Zoo, was returned to the Park and re-united with Katie. Their re-union, however, was to be short lived. Katie collapsed in her paddock, dying from heart failure – a terrible shock, for she was still a comparatively young animal. M'Tendre was not destined to be alone for very long. John Weatherhead went to Burma to collect Anna, Lucha and Kaylee, three young elephants who are being trained to give logging displays.

In 1989, Whipsnade contributed more to conservation than simply returning animals to the wild and supplying other collections; they helped preserve the dignity of the Kirghiz, a Turkish Mongolian people who had inhabited areas of Central Asia for centuries. After fighting against the Bolsheviks during the Russian Revolution, they were confined to a nomadic life in Afghanistan until the Russian invasion of that country, when they were forced to flee to Pakistan. Since the Turks consider all peoples who speak Turkic to belong to their nation, the Turkish Government airlifted the refugees, with what few possessions they could carry, to land in the Lake Van area, below Mount Ararat where, according to the Old Testament, Noah's Ark came to rest after the flood. Peter Somerville Large, a writer studying the Kirghiz, asked them what they missed most in their new home. Although they were no longer nomads, they replied 'Yaks'. For, during the nomadic lives of their forefathers, the yak provided wool, milk, flesh and hides, as well as being a beast of burden and fuelling their fires with its dried dung. Peter set about finding them some, since he felt their presence would renew the people's sense of dignity and history. On his return to England, he visited Richard Kock. There had always been yaks at Whipsnade – great shaggy creatures, whose birth

A Yak.   /BP

rate was among the highest and death rate one of the lowest in the Park. Richard selected two females and a male, but the male failed a test to qualify for export, so the females went on, not to the wild on the roof of the world, but to become domesticated among the Kirghiz once more.

Kashmir or Cashmere goats live in the Himalayan regions of India and Tibet and their silky underwool is used in the manufacture of high quality textiles. In 1828, George IV established a herd in Windsor Great Park. Now known as the 'Windsor White Goats', descendants of the Royal Kashmir herd were given into the keeping of the Zoological Society of London and have been quartered at Whipsnade since 1967. This herd provides mascots for Battalions of the Royal Regiment of Wales and the Welsh Fusiliers with such delightful names as Sospan, Dewii and Idris. Idris is wearing the official ceremonial Goat Coat of the 4th Battalion of the Royal Regiment of Wales and is pictured with two NCOs and keepers Marilyn Sudder, Graham Lucas, centre, and Pete Williams. /JH

CHAPTER 11

Scientific Developments

Many and varied are the creatures which have been hand-reared at Whipsnade, from baby elephants to a tiny Sever macaw, which was raised by Trevor Moxey who, I was told, must hold the record for the most successes. 'Who told you that?' he asked, with genuine surprise and modesty, when I tackled him on the subject whilst watching his

Trevor Moxey feeding a baby penguin. /DP

strong hands gently cradling a tiny, fluffy penguin chick, no bigger than a mouse, as he fed it carefully from a syringe. Then, he traced his finger along a strip of skin, now visible like a parting in the grey down on its tummy, stretched sufficiently for him to stop the feed and re-weigh the tiny creature on miniature scales. Pre- and post-feed weights were meticulously recorded before the little bird was popped back into the incubator.

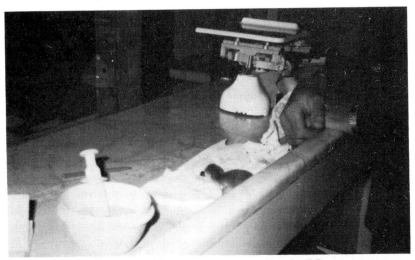

A two-day old Humboldt penguin.   /DP

Some three hundred and fifty Humboldt penguins have been hand reared since the early seventies by Trevor, Clive Bates, Bob Wingate and Andy White, among others. Trevor told me that it is necessary to hand rear Humboldts as they are not very good parents in captivity, tending to feed their young on all the wrong things, such as twigs, or whatever happens to be handy! The timing of the egg laying, therefore, is carefully monitored and the keepers are on stand-by to remove the chicks immediately they hatch, before the parents have the chance to give them even one feed. In the old days, when Trevor reared twelve chicks in tubs, in his coal barn at Chequers Cottages, they were given mashed sprats from a spoon. Now the sprats are liquidised with added 'Fish Eater Supplement' into a grey, very unappetising-looking sludge. Apart from Trevor's coal barn, chicks have been reared in the Old Pheasantry and the old Bakehouse, until it was incorporated into the Discovery Centre. Now, there is a purpose-built unit in the 'Care Centre', which was, until recently, the Children's Zoo. When penguins are between ten and fourteen days old, they graduate to 'solid food', strips of sprats, followed by whole sprats and, eventually, herring pieces. After being introduced to water, to thoroughly wet their feathers, they are, by three months old, ready to return to the colony on the Downs, or be sent to other collections.

It isn't only penguins though, that Trevor has brought up in his seventeen years at Whipsnade. Many wallabies have passed through his hands, or rather, his hat, for, according to him, an old hat inside a shopping basket or peg bag makes an ideal simulated pouch. Wallaby babies usually find themselves abandoned because, either they've fallen out of their mother's pouch when she has been startled, or the weather is too bad for her to cope, or she's been taken ill. There always seems to be a bright-eyed little wallaby head poking out of a bag or box in some corner of the Park or other. They are fed evaporated milk, watered down, since they find its sugar content difficult to digest, the strength gradually being increased with the quantity, although, over the last couple of years, an enzyme has been developed which helps with the digestion of the sugar intake. All the necessary 'Wallaby Vitamins' are added. Then, when the young animal is about six months old, it is let loose in the Park to revert to wallaby. They are emotional creatures, tending to develop an affinity for one person and, for this reason, they are always placed near another of their kind, on release.

On another occasion, Trevor announced that he was going to take a baby Chinese water deer home. Everyone told him there was no way he would succeed with the highly strung creature. Undeterred, he bedded it down near a radiator. Sensing that this particular animal needed a stable, tranquil environment, he left the radio playing softly in the background, day and night. Eventually he confounded the pessimists by returning the animal to the Park.

Charlie the muntjac had similar treatment. He listened to the radio for the first three weeks of his life, as well, before being returned to a heated stall, with food and water and an open door, so that, in his own good time, he could take himself off to join his fellows. First, however, he found the picnic area and begged for sandwiches. Not the most suitable fare for a muntjac, nor a wallaby, but keepers still tell of the one-eyed Nelson, who actually took a child's sandwich out of his hand before he could eat it! Cheeky Charlie went further than the picnic area and headed for the Estate Office where he soon discovered that he was on to a good thing. The girls, completely unable to resist his charms, fed him many tasty morsels. He then went on to rattle on the letterbox of a nearby house and when the keeper's wife opened the door, he made a bee-line for the kitchen. The great day came when he was destined to become a TV Star! Trevor had chosen him to appear on the 'Really Wild Show' as an ideal animal to illustrate how a baby, abandoned by its mother, can be reared and put back into the Park. He took Charlie home with him, intending to go straight to the Studio the following day. Charlie was by then six months old, but, much to the delight of Trevor's wife and children, he still remembered his way around the house where he had spent his first three weeks of life. Once more back at Whipsnade, with the added confidence of his television appearance, he set about wooing the female muntjacs. At least, that was what the keepers suspected when he turned up at the Children's Zoo, somewhat chastened and bruised. The other males, resenting his intrusion, had set about him. Feeling very sorry for himself, he spent the next few days curled up on the sofa in the keepers' quarters until he regained his equilibrium and set off into the Park once more.

Pippa's brief encounter with a muntjac. These little animals which roam freely in the Park can become quite tame. /DP

Sofas in the keepers' quarters! Lace curtains at the windows! A baby's cot in the corner of the Elephant keepers' room, where Sally Wood is hand-rearing Louie, the baby chimp! How those men of yesteryear would scoff at seeing such comforts. They who made do, at best, with a broken down old deck-chair and bedded baby animals in boxes. But this generation of keepers hasn't gone soft ... it's the face of keepering that has changed in more ways than one. Nowadays, a third of the animal carers at Whipsnade are women, working alongside the men on an equal footing, be it mucking out, hand rearing, training or observing and making notes about their charges.

In fact, it was one of 'Whipsnade's Women', who became the very first female Head Keeper at the London Zoo. 'How did they react to that up here?' I asked Linda Walker, as we stood in her London

Sally Wood mothering Louie.   /DP

With Linda Walker in her domain at the London Zoo.   /DP

169

Linda with a hand-reared London wallaby.   /DP

domain. 'A woman, and from Whipsnade too!' She laughed. Everyone had accepted her, she said; they had all been very helpful and there had been no resentment at all, not even from the men, that the only woman who'd applied had got the job. Perhaps her move was something they would have appreciated, it was people 'going down' to Whipsnade that they could never understand. Linda had been at Whipsnade for eighteen years, nine on the dolphins and the rest in the Children's Zoo, when, in 1987, the Headkeepership of the Regent's Park Children's Zoo had become vacant, and, feeling herself well qualified, she'd applied. 'Qualifications?' I asked. It transpired that Linda had been one of that very first group to take the 'Keepers' Course' at Paddington Tech., which had paved the way for the new breed of educated keeper.

Originally, as I have previously mentioned, no qualifications had been necessary to become a Zoo Keeper. A love of animals, an aptitude for hard work, joy at being in the open air in all weathers and a modicum of plain commonsense, being the only requirements. Now, as the general public becomes more wildlife and conservation conscious, more people want to work with animal collections, so, as the competition increases, higher standards are inevitably required from the applicants. These are vital, as the public becomes more informed, so the keepers must be able to talk to them more knowledgeably. Long gone are the days when, in response to 'D'yer wanner see it?' giggling girls trooped round the back of the Elephant House, to listen to the animal playing the mouth organ and put pennies into her trunk. It is a far cry from the early keeper who, when asked, 'Where are the urinals, my man?' replied, 'They 'aven't come down from London yet.' One member of staff told me that, at his interview some twenty years ago, all he was asked was 'Would you be prepared to get your hair cut?' and 'Could you put a bale of straw on your back and take it one pace forward and then slide back two?'

Now, the questions are more likely to be, 'How many GCSE's do you have?' One stands a better chance of acceptance if they are English, Maths and Science, especially Biology. Once taken on by the Society, the recruit is designated a 'Trainee Keeper' and training starts in earnest. As well as working on a section, the student attends lectures on subjects as varied as Health and Safety, Animal Handling and Budgeting! Previously, these were held in London, but it is far more cost effective to run separate courses at Whipsnade, withdrawing staff

The Waterhouse sisters, Leanne and Joanne, tell me about their training schedule. /DP

for the duration of one lecture, rather than sending them to London for the day. Visits to other collections are arranged during which other environments and husbandry are studied and compared. After two years, the Trainee sits a City & Guilds Examination, in London, which includes such questions as: Diets – Working with Dangerous Animals – Safety – Diagrams and Signs – Labelling – The Social Behaviour of Primates, etc. The successful candidate becomes a Qualified Keeper. Assessment of aptitude and practical work by the Head of Section and Region Overseer continue for the next four years, at the end of which another Exam is taken to qualify as a Senior Keeper. An integral part of this promotion is an 'in depth' interview with the Animal Manager and Director of Collections, two well qualified men, who consider the applicant's suitability, as well as knowledge. Following on, there are prospects for becoming Second in Charge of Section, Head of Section and, ultimately, an Overseer.

Occasionally, opportunities arise for exchanges with keepers in other countries. Two of Whipsnade's current staff, Alan Morris and Roger Catchpole, have availed themselves of this. Roger, who had nurtured schoolboy dreams of, one day, becoming a Game Warden, came to the Park in 1972, on the advice of his Biology teacher – to learn about animals! As it was for me – Whipsnade was destined to become *his* Africa – although he has paid an exchange visit to Toronto, with his wife, Anne, whom he met and fell in love with whilst working on the Rhino Section! In Toronto he recalls spending the long, hot summer outside in the African Paddock, whilst she stifled in the heat and humidity of the Indian and Malayan Pavilion. She, on the other hand, endured the harsh cold winter outside in the Canadian Domain, whilst he languished in the well-heated South American Pavilion. The greatest contrast between the two countries, he added, ruefully, was the salaries. It was hoped that one exchange might have gone on longer, but the visiting keeper just couldn't survive on the English wages, which were about half what he earned in Canada.

Perhaps the hardest thing for a parent to understand is a son or daughter, with three years at University and a Degree, or other excellent qualifications or skills, abandoning them, as they see it, 'just to muck out animals'! There is a great deal more to the job than the uninitiated expect. Each creature has to be inspected daily, to make sure it is in good health. Notes are made, records kept, behaviour carefully studied. Ask any of the staff why they came and they say it was love of animals or birds … ask them why they stay and they will, invariably, tell you that it is the love of the place and the job satisfaction that holds them like a spell. Why, it can't even be the uniform that attracts these days! In his youth, John Datlen was ribbed by the Works Staff that the reason he was taking a one pound a week drop in wages to become a keeper, was the uniform. That first uniform was very smart, consisting of a grey chauffeur-type suit and peaked cap. Alf Billington told me about a young lad who arrived one morning and was put to work alongside him. The next day the lad didn't turn up. His mother phoned instead. Her son wouldn't be coming to the 'Zoo' any more, she said ... He didn't like the dirty work. He hadn't expected to have to clean out the animal houses ... he wanted to wear a smart uniform, like Johnny Morris on the television!!!

Perhaps John Datlen knew what he was doing when he became a keeper. He is pictured here in the smart uniform of an Overseer. /DP

When Carla Tams first started at Whipsnade, the women wore grey trousers and jackets, like the men, but their uniforms were tailored and very flattering, she recalls, wistfully. The first break with the traditional was a move into bottle green, then jackets were abandoned in favour of olive green jumpers with buff shirts, black ties and shoes and olive trousers, only to be changed again later for brown trousers and shoes and open neck fawn coloured shirts. No doubt the men were glad to get out of the stiff-collared white shirts and hats and jackets which, no matter how hot the day, they were never allowed to remove. Perhaps, however, they are not so easily identifiable in their more casual outfits and my husband has, on occasion, been mistaken for one when wearing brown trousers, fawn shirt and an olive green body warmer. Even with the addition of brown zip jackets they are not as conspicuous as the vast army of Volunteers who stand out clearly from the crowd in their burgundy sweatshirts with 'Whipsnade Wild Animal Park' – 'Volunteer', emblazoned across their chests in white and the LifeWatch logo on their backs. Or on warmer days in their white T-Shirts with lettering and logo in burgundy.

'Vol' Walter Smith, a retired accountant, who saw an advert for 'Volunteers' in his local Berkhamsted paper. I met him first when he was on the 'Green Machine'. /DP

With funding always at a premium, these volunteers or 'Vols' as Margaret Williams, Education Officer, affectionately calls her brood, are invaluable to the Society. The Volunteers, who usually give their services for one day a week, between April and September, report to Graham Lucas at ten o'clock in the morning in his pre-fabricated office. Graham sorts out their duties for the day, which can be giving the commentary on the 'Great Whipsnade Railway', or manning any exhibitions which may be running, plus the Information Kiosk and the 'Green Machine'. This green painted van, which is taken on tours of the Park, was fitted out by the Vols themselves with animal skins, hooves, horns, antlers, etc. which visitors can touch. They take parties of schoolchildren on guided tours and supervise their brass rubbing and mask making. Training for the Vols, given by Margaret, is either on every other Sunday, during the first three months of the year, or on an intense, one week course in March, whichever suits them best. This training, which covers First Aid, The Animals in the Park, and simple

Biology is followed by a probationary period of sixty hours, after which they become Full Volunteers. Since the aim is for a body of seventy people, some with two years' experience are appointed Team Leaders.

Graham Lucas giving the 'Bear facts' on Lady Yule's Walk. Behind him is Flint Pit Paddock where Harry Rance narrowly missed being machine-gunned during the war.

/DP

At first I thought they were, in the main, retired people, pensioners who wanted an interest to keep mind and body active, or bored housewives with time on their hands. I was surprised to find that many have other jobs, some part time and others full time, giving up one of their days off. Peter Huggins had in fact once been a full time keeper until his financial commitments outstripped his salary and he, reluctantly, needed to find a better paid job. Now he comes back as a Vol on his day off! In return for the time they give, they are granted LifeWatch Membership, concessionary tickets to admit one adult or two children for every two days they put in at the Park, twenty percent discount on all non-consumable items in the Zoo Shop, use of the Staff Canteen and travel expenses of twenty pence per mile up to a maximum of six pounds, but, as they say, 'We don't do it for that, it's being here that counts!'

They also man the Discovery Centre, which was established as part of the Society's educational programme. The whole of the ground floor of the Old Hall Farm Building is used for this purpose, housing Man the Animal, the British Sea Shore, a South American Rain Forest and a darkened area with simulated night, so that nocturnal African Desert creatures can be seen. This Discovery Centre, which receives favourable comments from visitors from other collections, was opened by Sir David Attenborough, who has done so much to foster public interest in wild life. It will be remembered that, during the late sixties, the Federation of Zoological Gardens had wanted its member zoos to provide educational facilities. Whipsnade had had to shelve its plans, but now in the eighties an Education Centre materialised, although without its separate entrance, as had originally been planned. A pleasant school complex was created at the old Cloisters end of the Old Hall Farm building, in what had once been the Staff Canteen. There are two main rooms; the Classroom with tiered seating where children have 'Come and Touch' sessions, while Duchess the Lop Eared rabbit wanders at will, keeping an eye on the proceedings. The Lecture Room is well appointed, with Television and Film Projector. There can be up to five sessions a day, primarily for the five to nine age group. A few eleven to twelve years olds have lessons and experience with Classification, and some 'A' level pupils have lectures in subjects such as evolution. Margaret has also carried out an 'A' level study on 'Relating to Real Animals', in collaboration with Tring Natural History Museum. When she told me this, it reminded me of the Army Cadets, way back, who having recognised the stuffed animals round their camp had come to Whipsnade to experience the real thing.

All that had happened towards the close of the eighties decade left me with no doubt in my mind that Whipsnade Wild Animal Park had achieved even more than Sir Peter had ever dreamed. Yet, although all seemed to be going well on the surface, an air of foreboding hung over the Park as the eighties drew to a close. No one knew what its future was to be … if, indeed, it was to have a future! Rumours abounded, each one more depressing than the last.

On the 125th Anniversary of Sir Peter's birth, I stood on a mound of earth, hardly able to believe that I was actually standing on top of the deep pit that had once been home to tigers and, later, Kodiak bears. To my right, all traces of the Polar Bear Pen were eradicated! Times were so hard, the Society had allowed a contractor to get rid of unwanted topsoil by filling them in, together with all the old flint pits along the face of the Downs. During that hot, dry summer of 1989 even Ouseley Pond, Sir Peter's 'Fairy Pool', had dried up for the very first time in living memory. Was it an omen, I wondered? Was this, his dream, about to disappear from the face of the earth, along with his Tiger Pit?

CHAPTER 12

Into the Future

The January gales of 1990 had swept through the Park, tearing up well over sixty mature trees and demolishing Cut Throat and Holly Frindle shelters. In the devastation, Roopa, the Great Indian rhino, comforted her three month old calf, Bardia, while Primrose, the chimpanzee, cast off her newest baby, Louie. The keepers found the little scrap of black fur abandoned on the floor of his pen, clutching at some wool for comfort. Normally mother chimps have a space of about six years between babies, but Primrose had had four in ten. Paco, the first second-generation chimp in any British zoo, having been born the year before the Golden Jubilee, was followed four years later by Nikki, then Wally, in 1987, and now Louie. Young chimps still need some of their mother's attention until they are almost seven, so, no doubt, the poor creature must have felt she couldn't cope again. The keepers gently carried the unwanted little animal to their quarters beside the Elephant House where newly arrived Trainee Keeper, Sally Wood, took him under her wing and into her heart.

There were two brief glimmers of hope in the wake of the gales. During the past five years, over four thousand trees of seventy-two species had been planted in the Park, many donated by 'Men of Trees'. Many saplings had been spared and amidst the devastation in Duke's Avenue clusters of fragile snowdrops stood defiantly in the rain, their tiny, pointed leaves like little spears of hope, pointing to a brighter future.

I, for one, had no idea just how bright that future was to be. Between January and Easter, I visited the London Zoo, where a tremendous work schedule was going ahead. I suspected that it had received the lion's share of the Government's last and final grant of ten million pounds, for, in my mind, Whipsnade had always been the poor relation, receiving the crumbs that London could spare, since I'd noted as a child, that whenever they had a new lorry, the old one had been passed down to us! This time, I discovered, to my delight, that I was wrong. Because, after Easter, I returned to Whipsnade Wild Animal Park, hoping against hope that it would survive, knowing that at least the daffodils would be nodding their golden trumpets to cheer my day with their promise of spring. Totally unexpected though, were the bright banners fluttering from tall white flagpoles at the approach to the Main Gate. Long, narrow banners with abstract designs, depicting animal skins: Cheetah – Zebra – Reptile – Tiger – Giraffe and the electric blue of Kingfisher or the Peacock whose raucous voice welcomed us into the Park. A Park that had dramatically changed its image with its smart new logo and its new style signs. Another wind had followed hard upon the gales. The wind of change had swept through Whipsnade Park.

Totally unexpected were the banners fluttering from the tall flagpoles. /DP

How quickly it had all happened! The devastation of the gales was gone, the trunks of felled trees attractively utilised. Two new shelters had arisen from the splinters of Cut Throat and Holly Frindle, smart new buildings in the style of modern log cabins. In some strangely unexpected way the colourful new signposts enhanced the landscape with which they blended so beautifully. The whole of this new 'Corporate Image', designed by Stewart and Knight, from the 'panethnic' designs of the flags – repeated like a row of tails on headed notepaper and publications – to the lettering on the sides of the smart cream and brown vehicles, conveys a new, lively and exciting 'Wild

Animal Park'. Gone is the slightly outdated image of the past, yet all has been changed so tastefully, that surely no-one, however seriously minded, could find any of it objectionable. In fact, it seems to me the whole place has come alive in a vibrant way, as never before in its history.

The new image.   /DP

Trail Breaker, the smart new 1990s road train offers free rides all day, stopping at Rhinos Crash, Cheetahs Leap, Owls Stare, Ducks Plump, Wolves Rout and Hippos Wallow.   */DP*

179

The changes have even brought a sparkle back to the Old Hall
Farm, for, rather than standing out starkly against its changed
background, the mellow red brick building seems to glow contentedly
amidst its new surroundings; and what strange new surroundings they
are! The Bird Sanctuary nearby, which had always been a Sanctuary –
visitors being only allowed in accompanied by a keeper in small

The Bird Sanctuary has been opened up.   /DP

parties – has become a Bird Walk with new paths carved through its
undergrowth and rhododendron bushes. Across Central Avenue, a
huge mound of earth has risen on the Great Lawn in front of the
Elephant House. On closer inspection, it is seen to be the banking of a
semi-circular Amphitheatre, where Kaylee, Lucha and Anna will
eventually demonstrate their skills at logging. Being the offspring of
working animals, they take naturally to pushing and rolling logs,
something they spend many happy hours doing, when not playing with
their big red ball and not immersed in the water of their pool. It is the
keepers, Graham Frost and Dave Fisher who, not being the children of
mahouts, are having to master the art of riding and controlling the
elephants before the displays can begin! All extra training must be
fitted into their busy schedule, when there are no visitors about.

Here two brightly coloured macaws, Whipsnade's own 'Red Arrows', fly past in formation. An owl swoops overhead in silent flight. Yet another Jacko, this time a kookaburra, wrestles noisily with his keeper for his rubber snake, his rasping voice making it easy to understand how the kookaburra earned the nickname 'laughing jackass'. The birds on display vary from performance to performance and are trained and exhibited by Southern Californian, David Frank, the Park's Events Manager, assisted by Gordon Mellor and Andy Reeve. /DP

David Frank – Events Manager. /DP

181

Salt, Pepper and Berkeley.   */DP*

A sea lion leaps as elegantly as any dolphin.   */DP*

Jane Pardoe tells me of her parents' reactions when, after having taken a degree in Zoology, she announced she was going to become a keeper! /DP

Nigel Williams who decided when his house in Australia burned down that he would make a long anticipated trip to Britain. Since his job back home had been taking reptiles into schools, he applied to zoos and collections and Chris Webster snapped him up for Whipsnade, where during the summer of 1990 he presents the sea lion exhibition with Jane Pardoe and Joan Crabtree. /DP

What a pity visitors can no longer savour the delight of the swaying ride on an elephant's back. A whole generation is growing up which has never known this thrill ... and it's very expensive to go to India, or Thailand, or Burma. My older children, Rebecca and Paul, who are, incidentally, two of the very few human beings actually to have been born in the Park, loved the rides, till they were stopped. Pippa and Bill not only missed the 'kudos' of being born in the Park, they missed the elephant rides as well.

On the other side of Central Avenue, beyond a second Amphitheatre for the Birds of Prey Presentation, two tiny sealions, Salt and Pepa, train alongside enormous, experienced Berkeley in the art of balancing balls on their noses and catching hoops on their necks. Skills which are expertly demonstrated daily by Liz, June and Ben, who leap to touch the suspended ball as easily and elegantly as any dolphin ever did. There is such a radiance about these sea mammals as they perform, they seem to enjoy the appreciative adulation of their audience as much as the tasty morsels of fish which are their reward.

Pointed wooden turrets, silhouetted against the greenery of the trees, are just visible over the parapet wall. Shrieks of childish delight pierce the air as small bodies hurtle headlong down the large silver tubes attached to the sides of the Towers. For this is the imaginative new play area which Paul's two children, Heidi and Mark, think is 'wicked!', 'cool!' ... a few yards away the old, mundane slide stands deserted. Swings hang idle as the new generation fling themselves across the Aerial Runway, or scramble up and down the flexible climbing frames in 'Running Wild', whilst their parents can relax for a while beneath the horse chestnut trees, or wander to the 'Café by the Lake', the romantic new name for Avenue Kiosk, standing as it does, so close to the Navy's Lake Daedulus. Here the Railway chugs past on its way to 'Asia', where the two-humped, Bactrian camels, whose ancestors came from a region of Afghanistan between the Hindu Kush Mountains and the River Oxus, shelter beneath the trees from the heat of the day. One solitary ankole, who has somehow strayed into another Continent, stands contentedly amongst the grazing yaks.

Behind the fine herd of Père David deer, another man-made hill is rising. Will this project, I wonder, run right into Sir Peter's Way? Will the Dagnall Gate ever materialise? Will Sir Peter's tomb overlook a new way into the Park? What will happen to the large flat area at Icknield Gate, when the contract with those who organise the Site Equipment Exhibitions runs out? Will it ever become Sir Peter's dreamed-of Lake? Whatever does eventually happen to it, I'm sure it will be used wisely and well!!

Owen Chamberlain, now the New Projects Manager, was busy marking out the line of a path sweeping from the Hall Farm complex, round the Greater Flamingoes' Pond and into the Chartley Paddock, where the domestic cattle of that name had been one of the first species that Whipsnade had preserved from extinction. How apt, I felt, that a field with such a record should have been chosen for the new Children's Farm Exhibit. Owen nodded towards the fine new towers in 'Running Wild'. 'We had a bit of trouble assembling those,' he said; it seemed that the Scandinavian manufacturers had given him the impression that the whole operation was so simple, 'Any child could do it!' 'Trouble was,' added Owen 'I only had men!' We looked, admiringly, at the Shire horse grazing under a nearby tree. John Datlen was very pleased with himself. He'd run an old farm wagon to earth. It needed renovating and re-painting. One can feel the enthusiasm generated by all that is happening. So different from the sense of apprehension and foreboding which hung over everyone last year. The Park has come alive and its staff is responding to the lead. The dynamism is infectious.

It seems my fears of the previous year were well founded. The Zoological Society of London had seriously contemplated off-loading its country annexe which, although renowned throughout the world for its successes in breeding endangered species, had not been paying its way for years. In 1989, a spokesman had told the press that Whipsnade needed six hundred thousand visitors a year to break even. In that year, only some four hundred and forty-two thousand, six hundred passed through its gates. The Zoological Society had realised that 'cut-throat' times were here. Although, as a nation, our leisure time and our mobility to enjoy it were increasing, so were the numbers of attractions vying for our patronage. If it was to compete successfully in this new climate, the advice of the Leisure industry's professionals was essential. The Society sought the expertise of the Grant Leisure Group, one of the foremost operators in the country. Together with the Council of the Zoological Society, Zoo Operations Ltd. was formed to, once more, bring the Society back from the brink of bankruptcy.

They took a long hard look at Whipsnade Wild Animal Park and assessed its value to the Society. On the purely practical side, London, in spite of all the new improvements, will still be, basically, a Victorian zoo, a place where scientists, artists and the general public can get a good look at exotic animals at close quarters. These animals cannot always be kept in what are today considered ethically acceptable conditions. There is no possibility of the Zoo being allowed to encroach further into the adjacent Regent's Park. At Whipsnade they possess vast acres of land. Surely here lay the future? All the 'country cousin' needed was a face lift and a programme to publicise its new image as successfully as its uniqueness had been put across at its opening. For, in 1931, Whipsnade was the first country Zoo in the world, opened long before any of the Safari Parks. In fact, if Whipsnade hadn't proved that wild animals from alien climates could adapt, survive and breed in our fickle English climate, would any of these other places ever have come into being? Its fame had spread to such an extent that during the war I received a letter from a cousin in Canada, addressed simply to Whipsnade Park, Nr. Dunstable, Beds. No mention of England or the UK at all. Luton was, in its pre-airport days, described as a small, hat manufacturing town near Whipsnade Park!

Tilak Suriya had heard of it in Sri Lanka, long before he came over to help with the elephants in 1967. Since then he has travelled all over the world and now, back once more for the summer, he told me he has

With Tilak Suriya.   /DP

186

discovered for himself just how unique Whipsnade still is. His dark eyes shine as he says, 'It is one on its own. Its location, its layout; and wherever I have been in zoological circles, anywhere in the world, they have all heard of Whipsnade Park.' I was so glad to hear what, in my heart, I had hoped to be true. I was scandalised a few weeks later to meet a young man in Somerset, wearing a tie with a cheetah printed on it, who had never heard of either Whipsnade Wild Animal Park or its successful breeding cheetahs, Juanita and Jack. He knows about them now.

'Fortunately for the Park, alternative thinking prevailed,' Chris Webster, the newly appointed Operations Manager, told me as we sat in his light airy office. This slim ex-army Captain is as unlike the portly Captain Beal as the new Whipsnade is as unlike the Country Estate he managed sixty years ago. Instead of selling Whipsnade off, Andy Grant, the Managing Director of Zoo Operations Ltd. and the Grant Leisure Group, sent Andrew Forbes, one of his chief personnel

'The A Team'. Left Chris Webster, Operations Manager, centre Owen Chamberlain, New Projects Manager, right Richard Kock, Animal Manager /JH

*Roy Thomas, Marketing Manager, to the left of the group and Chris Packham from the
'Really Wild Show', welcoming the 30 millionth visitor in the Park's history on May
Day Saturday 1990.* /DP

who had been advising at the London Zoo, down to Whipsnade to take
on the role of Chief Executive. Andrew Forbes gathered a lively,
experienced team around him. Richard Kock, with his excellent
veterinary qualifications, became the Animal Manager. Owen
Chamberlain, with his extensive knowledge of the Park and its work
force, took on the newly created post of New Projects Manager. Lewis
Killon came from Leeds Castle to take over as Catering Manager,
when the J Lyons franchise ended. Roy Thomas was recruited as
Marketing Manager. Already his brief television advertising campaign
on Central TV prior to the May Day weekend accounted for
twenty-four percent of the visitors who came to see for themselves
'Out of Africa Out of Bedfordshire' in what was an African
celebration month. For me, that Saturday morning, in the burning heat,
with bearded Charles Whitbread, Roy's assistant, resplendent in safari
suit, talking to the African Dancers before they performed in the
Elephant Amphitheatre; the beat of the drums, ethnic arts and crafts for
sale and two mock native mud huts – Whipsnade truly symbolised 'My
Africa'.

I met Andrew Forbes and he told me of some of his ideas and aims
for the future. Judging by the performance of his team so far,

Whipsnade looks to be set on course for a vivid, lively future, filled with ever increasing interest for the vast number of visitors it needs to survive. Survive it will, if you, dear reader, come and come again, come to this place, which, while not a Pleasure Park as such, offers infinite pleasure to a far wider section of the public than any ordinary Pleasure Park. Nor is it a Theme Park, yet it has the greatest theme of all, that of conservation. Together with the London Zoo, these two great National Parks carry out scientific research and field studies that benefit the animal kingdom all over the world. Whatever happens, this cannot be allowed to fail.

Bob Wingate, Head of the Discovery Centre, with part of a tree which he says will be ideal for the new Golden Lion tamarins, two of which have been sent from the Jersey Wildlife Reservation. The general public may not find them as entertaining as the marmosets they are replacing but they are an endangered species which is slowly being rescued. To enhance the project Kew Gardens have sent plants indigenous to the small monkeys' native homeland, the Atlantic Rain Forest of Brazil. I found the collaboration between Kew and Whipsnade thrilling. It had always been the dream of Sir Stamford Raffles, 1721–1826, the founder of Singapore and the London Zoo to establish a Zoological Society to help the development of zoology in the way the Horticultural Society was aiding botany. Kew Gardens, founded by King George III's mother, were given to the nation by Queen Victoria in 1840. Sadly, Sir Stamford Raffles died almost two years before the opening of the London Zoo in April 1828, but the Zoological Society which he worked so hard to establish surely aids zoology throughout the world in ways he could never have imagined. /DP

So what can you, who truly care what happens to the wild life of this world, do to help? You can join LifeWatch, the Society's new membership scheme which has replaced Friends of the Zoo. Your subscription will help towards the funding of new projects. In return, you will receive a magazine that keeps you up to date with the zoological affairs of the two collections, you will be allowed to attend

With Teddy (on the seat donated by Captain Beal's family in his memory) – facing Sir Peter's memorial plinth on the approach to Hall Farm. /DP

seminars and lectures, if you so wish, but, perhaps more importantly for you, you will have free access to the London Zoo and Whipsnade Wild Animal Park as often as you wish throughout the year.

For Whipsnade is not just a summer place. Sir Peter showed it to the Council on a November day as the sun burned through the swirling mists in the valley below. I have described the sheer beauty of a tiger's fur against the stark whiteness of snow. In spring, young animals gaze with wonder at the bright, new world into which they have been born, young wallabies poke their heads out of their mother's pouches as they lurk among the daffodils. Muntjacs and Chinese Water deer thread their way through the hyacinth haze of Bluebell Wood, peacocks fan out their gorgeous feathers as they woo their mates.

Sir Peter wrote at its inception that 'The (Zoological) Society will be content if, at its second century in 2029, its wise foresight will be applauded and its plans prove to have been well and truly made.' How he, who joined the Society himself in 1903 to pull it out of bankruptcy and came up with the idea of Whipsnade Park, would approve of all the efforts that are now being made to perpetuate his dream.

WILD ANIMAL PARK

Whipsnade is home to over 2,800 animals and is the UK's largest conservation centre specialising in the breeding of rare and endangered species such as cheetahs, rhinos and scimitar-horned oryx.

BECOME A LIFEWATCH FRIEND
and benefit from:

■ ▶◀ ■

membership card entitling you to free admission to Whipsnade Wild Animal Park and London Zoo for one year

■ ▶◀ ■

free subscription to "Lifewatch" Magazine for one year (3 editions)

■ ▶◀ ■

four vouchers entitling your guests to 50p off the cost of admission to Whipsnade Wild Animal Park or London Zoo

■ ▶◀ ■

"Lifewatch" car sticker

■ ▶◀ ■

discount on items purchased in the shop.

For further information enquire at the Lifewatch centre, Whipsnade shop or telephone (0582) 872171

SPECIAL EVENTS
take place on several weekends throughout the year — full details on request.

LIFE*WATCH*
Every living thing is our concern

Books Published by
THE BOOK CASTLE

NORTH CHILTERNS CAMERA, 1863–1954; FROM THE THURSTON COLLECTION IN LUTON MUSEUM:
edited by Stephen Bunker
Rural landscapes, town views, studio pictures and unique royal portraits by the area's leading early photographer.

THROUGH VISITORS' EYES: A BEDFORDSHIRE ANTHOLOGY:
edited by Simon Houfe
Impressions of the county by famous visitors over the last four centuries, thematically arranged and illustrated with line drawings.

JOURNEYS INTO BEDFORDSHIRE: Anthony Mackay
Foreword by The Marquess of Tavistock
A lavish book of over 150 evocative ink drawings.

FOLK: CHARACTERS and EVENTS in the HISTORY of BEDFORDSHIRE and NORTHAMPTONSHIRE: Vivienne Evans
Arranged by village/town, an anthology of stories about the counties' most intriguing historical figures.

ECHOES: TALES and LEGENDS of BEDFORDSHIRE and HERTFORDSHIRE: Vic Lea
Thirty, compulsively retold historical incidents.

TERESA of WATLING STREET: Arnold Bennett
Introduced by Simon Houfe
The only detective story by one of the twentieth century's most famous novelists. Written and set in Bedfordshire.

A LASTING IMPRESSION: Michael Dundrow
An East End boy's wartime experiences as an evacuee on a Chilterns farm at Totternhoe.

JOHN BUNYAN: HIS LIFE and TIMES: Vivienne Evans
Foreword by the Bishop of Bedford
Bedfordshire's most famous son set in his seventeenth century context.

LOCAL WALKS: NORTH and MID-BEDFORDHSIRE: Vaughan Basham
Twenty five circular walks, each linked to an interesting topic.

LOCAL WALKS: SOUTH BEDFORDSHIRE and NORTH CHILTERNS: Vaughan Basham
Twenty seven thematic circular walks.

DUNSTABLE DECADE: THE EIGHTIES = A collection of photographs: Pat Lovering
A souvenir book of nearly 300 pictures of people and events in the 1980s.

DUNSTABLE IN DETAIL: Nigel Benson
A hundred of the town's buildings and features, past and present, plus town-trail map.

OLD DUNSTABLE: Bill Twaddle
A new edition of this collection of early photographs.

BOURNE AND BRED: A DUNSTABLE BOYHOOD BETWEEN THE WARS: Colin Bourne
An elegantly-written, well-illustrated book capturing the spirit of the town over fifty years ago.

ROYAL HOUGHTON: Pat Lovering
Illustrated history of Houghton Regis from the earliest times to the present day.

OLD HOUGHTON, INCLUDING UPPER HOUGHTON, NOW PART OF DUNSTABLE: Pat Lovering
Over 170 photographs of Houghton Regis during the last 100 years.

Specially for Children

ADVENTURE ON THE KNOLLS: A STORY OF IRON AGE BRITAIN: Michael Dundrow
Excitement on Totternhoe Knolls as ten-year-old John finds himself back in those dangerous times, confronting Julius Caesar and his army.

THE RAVENS: ONE BOY AGAINST THE MIGHT OF ROME: James Dyer
On the Barton hills and in the south-east of England as the men of the great fort of Ravensburgh (near Hexton) confront the invaders.

Further titles are in preparation.

All the above are available via any bookshop,
or from the publisher and bookseller

THE BOOK CASTLE
12 Church Street, Dunstable, Bedfordshire LU5 4RU, Tel (0582) 605670